Revelation 20
and the Millennial Debate

Matthew Waymeyer

Kress Christian
PUBLICATIONS

Published by:

Kress Christian
PUBLICATIONS
P.O. Box 132228
The Woodlands, TX 77393
www.kresschristianpublications.com

ISBN 0-9717568-8-0

Cover Design: Paul Lewis

Introduction

This book arose from my own quest to understand what the Bible teaches about eschatology. Having read a number of works dealing with the end times from a systematic perspective, I decided to embark on an exegetical study of various key passages that addressed the questions swirling around in my mind. This, I decided, would enable me to lay a foundation for my own understanding of Scripture's teaching about the future. Revelation 20 was one of these passages, and this book is the fruit of my study of this crucial chapter.

A word about the format. *Revelation 20 and the Millennial Debate* reads much like a syllabus, and that's because it is, or at least it was. It began as a paper I wrote while studying at The Master's Seminary, and then it evolved into a class I taught at the Logos Bible Institute (a ministry of Grace Community Church in Sun Valley, California). Its current form is very similar to what I handed out to my students in that class. The strength of this format, I believe, is that it sets forth the various views—and arguments for those views—in a manner that is easy for the reader to follow.

In this way, the primary contribution of this book rests not so much in the area of original thought as in its presentation of the arguments of writers who have gone before. In discussing the major interpretive issues in Revelation 20, I have tried to be fair in setting forth each of the various positions. For this reason, even those who disagree with my conclusions should find it helpful. As you read, may the Lord bless you with a clearer understanding of His plan for the future and a joyful anticipation of the grace to be given you at the revelation of Jesus Christ.

Contents

Chapter 1
Introduction to Eschatology and the Question of the Millennium

Introduction to Eschatology

I. What is Eschatology?

"Eschatology" comes from the Greek word meaning "last" and refers to the study of "last things"—those future events that will take place at the consummation of the present age. Eschatology, then, is the study of what is commonly referred to as the "end times," and it involves issues such as the rapture of the saints, the Second Coming of Christ, the future resurrection, the final judgment, and the eternal state.

II. Why Study Eschatology?

Although many people are fascinated with the study of eschatology for the wrong reasons, there are many profitable reasons for engaging in such a study. The most significant one is that a contemplation of future events in God's plan fosters an expectancy that prepares one's heart for a life of worship, joy, and obedience (Titus 2:11-14; 2 Pet 3:14; 1 Pet 1:3-6, 13-16; 1 John 3:2-3; Phil 3:17-21; 2 Cor 4:16-18; 5:9-10; Rom 8:18-25; 11:33-36; 12:12a; Heb 10:24-25). As someone once said, "Bible prophecy is not given so we make a *calendar*—it's given to mold our *character*."

The Question of the Millennium

The word "millennium" means "one thousand years," and—in biblical and theological contexts—it refers to the thousand-year period spoken of in Revelation 20. One of the most significant theological questions concerning the millennium is when it will occur in relation to the Second Coming of Christ. Three primary theological positions have arisen to answer this question—premillennialism, postmillennialism, and amillennialism.

I. Premillennialism

Premillennialism is the view that Christ will return *before* the millennium (the prefix "pre-" means "before").[1]

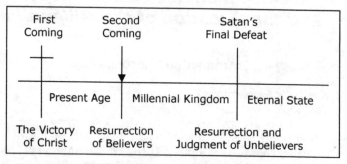

According to premillennialism:

A. The present age will climax with a period of Great Tribulation and the Second Coming of Christ.

B. When Christ returns, He will establish an earthly kingdom and rule over it for a thousand-year period often known as the *millennium*.

   1. At the time of Christ's return, believers will be resurrected to reign with Him, and Satan will be bound in the abyss where he will remain for the thousand years.

   2. During the millennium, Christ will reign in righteousness and there will be peace and justice throughout the earth.

2

C. At the end of the thousand years, Satan will be released from the abyss and will gather the remaining unbelievers for battle against Christ, but they will be decisively defeated.

D. All unbelievers will then be raised from the dead, and God will judge them according to their deeds.

E. After this final judgment, both believers and unbelievers will enter the eternal state.

II. Postmillennialism

Postmillennialism is the view that Christ will return *after* the millennium (the prefix "post-" means "after").

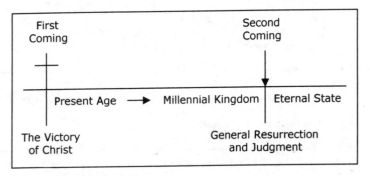

According to postmillennialism:

A. Through the proclamation of the gospel in the present age, an unprecedented number of people in the world—in fact, a vast majority—will turn to Christ and be saved.

   1. This time of mass spiritual expansion of God's kingdom—often called the *millennium*—is not seen as the entire period of time between the first and second comings of Christ.

   2. Instead, it is believed that the present age gradually merges into the millennium in such a way that it is difficult, if not impossible, to discern the exact starting point of the millennium.

B. The millennium will be characterized by spiritual prosperity, universal peace and righteousness, and economic well-being. Although Christ is not physically present on earth during this millennial period, He is believed to be the primary agent and cause of the church's expansion and influence.

C. At the end of the millennium, there will be a brief period of apostasy and conflict between the church and the forces of evil. This will be followed by the return of Christ and the resurrection and judgment of all mankind, who will then enter the eternal state.

III. Amillennialism

Amillennialism is the view that there will be *no* future millennium in the sense that the pre- or postmillennialists teach (the prefix "a-" means "not"). In other words, the present age *is* the millennial kingdom.

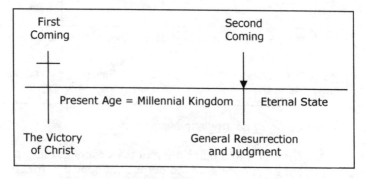

According to amillennialism:

A. The millennial kingdom—which was inaugurated by Christ's victory at the cross—began at the first coming of Christ and will continue until the time of His Second Coming.

B. The millennial kingdom is—and will continue to be—characterized by a mixture of good and evil.

C. The conflict between good and evil will intensify toward the end of the present age, and the increasing persecution will culminate in the appearance of the antichrist and the Second Coming of Christ.

D. When Christ returns, there will be a general resurrection and judgment of both believers and unbelievers, after which both will be ushered into the eternal state.

A Summary Comparison of the Millennial Views

Pre: Present Age // 2nd Coming // Millennial Kingdom

Post: Present Age ⟶ Millennial Kingdom // 2nd Coming

A: Present Age = Millennial Kingdom // 2nd Coming

Conclusion

Although there are many issues that fall in the area of eschatology, the question of the millennium is one of the most significant and hotly debated. Perhaps no other passage in Scripture speaks as directly to the issue of the relative timing of the millennium as Revelation 20.

Chapter 2
Introduction to the Book of Revelation

The Background of Revelation

Before considering a passage of Scripture, it is helpful to consider the background of the book in which it occurs.

I. The Author of Revelation

    The author of Revelation is the apostle John, who refers to himself as the author four times in the book (1:1, 4, 9; 22:8).

II. The Date of Revelation

    Revelation was written in the last decade of the first century (A.D. 94-96), near the end of the reign of Emperor Domitian (A.D. 81-96). Although some have argued that Revelation was written near the end of the reign of Nero (A.D. 54-68), evidence for the later date is strong.[2]

III. The Occasion of Revelation

    John wrote Revelation while in exile on the small and barren Island of Patmos, which is located in the Aegean Sea, southwest of Ephesus. The apostle had been banished there by the Roman authorities because of his faithfulness in proclaiming the gospel (1:9). While he was on Patmos, John received a series of visions, which he was faithful to record in the book of Revelation.

IV. The Recipients of Revelation

The book of Revelation is addressed to seven churches in Asia Minor (1:4, 11; 2:1-3:22; 22:16), which is part of modern-day Turkey. Some of these believers were already facing persecution; for others, persecution was just around the corner (1:9; 2:9-10, 13).

V. The Purpose of Revelation

The purpose of the book of Revelation is to instill hope in believers by fixing their eyes on the Lord's sovereign control over the world and His ultimate victory over evil.

An Overview of Revelation

I. A General Outline of Revelation

Many interpreters have drawn outlines of the book from the three direct objects in Revelation 1:19: "Write therefore (a) the things which you have seen, and (b) the things which are, and (c) the things which shall take place."

A. The Things You Have Seen (1)

B. The Things That Are Now (2-3)

   1. The Church in Ephesus (2:1-7)

   2. The Church in Smyrna (2:8-11)

   3. The Church in Pergamum (2:12-17)

   4. The Church in Thyatira (2:18-29)

   5. The Church in Sardis (3:1-6)

   6. The Church in Philadelphia (3:7-13)

   7. The Church in Laodicea (3:14-22)

C. The Things of the Future (4-22)

    1. The Two Scenes of Heavenly Preparation (4:1-5:14)

        a. The First Scene (4:1-11)

        b. The Second Scene (5:1-14)

    2. The Seven Seals (6:1-8:5)

        a. The First Seal (6:1-2)

        b. The Second Seal (6:3-4)

        c. The Third Seal (6:5-6)

        d. The Fourth Seal (6:7-8)

        e. The Fifth Seal (6:9-11)

        f. The Sixth Seal (6:12-17)

        g. Interlude: The Redeemed of the Great Tribulation (7)

        h. The Seventh Seal (8:1-5)

    3. The Seven Trumpets (8:6-11:19)

        a. The First Trumpet (8:6-7)

        b. The Second Trumpet (8:8-9)

        c. The Third Trumpet (8:10-11)

        d. The Fourth Trumpet (8:12)

        e. The Fifth Trumpet (8:13-9:12)

        f. The Sixth Trumpet (9:13-21)

        g. Interlude: The Little Book and the Witnesses (10:1-11:14)

    h. The Seventh Trumpet (11:15-19)

4. The Seven Signs (12:1-14:20)

    a. The Woman and the Dragon (12:1-17)

    b. The Two Beasts (13:1-18)

    c. The Lamb and the 144,000 (14:1-5)

    d. The Harvest of the Earth (14:6-20)

5. The Seven Bowls (15:1-19:10)

    a. The Heavenly Preparation (15:1-8)

    b. The First Bowl (16:1-2)

    c. The Second Bowl (16:3)

    d. The Third Bowl (16:4-7)

    e. The Fourth Bowl (16:8-9)

    f. The Fifth Bowl (16:10-11)

    g. The Sixth Bowl (16:12-16)

    h. The Seventh Bowl (16:17-19:10)

6. The Consummation of All Things (19:11-22:21)

    a. The Second Coming of Christ (19:11-21)

    b. The Millennial Reign of Christ (20:1-6)

    c. The Final Defeat of Satan (20:7-10)

    d. The White Throne of Judgment (20:11-15)

    e. The New Heaven and the New Earth (21:1-22:21)

II. Interpretive Approaches to Revelation 6-18

Although the entire book of Revelation is difficult to interpret, chapters 6-18 propose a unique challenge. In seeking to understand the meaning of this section of Revelation, scholars have, for the most part, taken one of the four following approaches—the idealist approach, the preterist approach, the historicist approach, or the futurist approach.

A. The Idealist Approach

According to the idealist approach, the visions of Revelation 6-18 do not relate to any historical events at all, but only symbolize the ongoing struggle between good and evil during the church age until Christ returns.

B. The Preterist Approach

According to the preterist approach, the visions of Revelation 6-18 describe events wholly limited to John's own time. In other words, everything described in these chapters took place in the first century.

C. The Historicist Approach

According to the historicist approach, the visions of Revelation 6-18 refer to actual events that take place throughout church history, that is, from the beginning of the church until the time of the modern interpreter.

D. The Futurist Approach

According to the futurist approach—which is reflected in the outline provided above—the visions of Revelation 6-18 relate to a period immediately preceding the Second Coming of Christ at the end of the age. This approach is reflected in the outline provided above.

Regardless of the approach taken by various interpreters, it is agreed that chapter 20 contains key teaching in the area of eschatology.

Introduction to the Millennium
of Revelation 20:1-6

I. The millennium of verses 1-6, in particular, has been the subject of a great deal of discussion and disagreement.

Revelation 20:1-6

(1) And I saw an angel coming down from heaven, having the key of the abyss and a great chain in his hand. (2) And he laid hold of the dragon, the serpent of old, who is the devil and Satan, and bound him for a thousand years, (3) and threw him into the abyss, and shut it and sealed it over him, so that he should not deceive the nations any longer, until the thousand years were completed; after these things he must be released for a short time.

(4) And I saw thrones, and they sat upon them, and judgment was given to them. And I saw the souls of those who had been beheaded because of the testimony of Jesus and because of the word of God, and those who had not worshiped the beast or his image, and had not received the mark upon their forehead and upon their hand; and they came to life and reigned with Christ for a thousand years. (5) The rest of the dead did not come to life until the thousand years were completed. This is the first resurrection. (6) Blessed and holy is the one who has a part in the first resurrection; over these the second death has no power, but they will be priests of God and of Christ and will reign with Him for a thousand years.

II. The various interpretations of Revelation 20:1-6 seek to answer five crucial questions:

A. Is the binding of Satan present or future?

B. Is the "first resurrection" spiritual or physical?

C. Is the duration of the thousand years symbolic or literal?

D. Is the locale of the millennial reign heaven or earth?

E. Is the chronology of Revelation 19:21-20:1 recapitulatory or sequential?

A Summary of Key Interpretive Issues in Rev 20:1-6			
Issue	Premil	Postmil	Amil
Satan's Binding:	Future	Present/Future	Present
First Resurrection:	Physical	Spiritual	Spiritual
Thousand Years:	Literal	Literal/Symbolic	Symbolic
Locale of Reign:	Earth	Earth/Heaven	Heaven
Chronology of 19-20:	Sequential	Sequ/Recap	Recap

III. These five questions will be addressed in chapters 3-7, and Revelation 20:7-15 will be addressed in chapters 8 and 9.

Chapter 3
The Timing of Satan's Binding: Present or Future?

The Significance of the Question

One of the key interpretive issues in Revelation 20 is the timing of Satan's binding in verses 1-3. Is Satan currently bound as recorded in this passage, or does the fulfillment of that vision await a future time? If Satan is presently bound, the millennial kingdom of Revelation 20 is a present reality, but if Satan's binding is yet future, so is the millennial kingdom. Amillennialists and many postmillennialists believe it is present, and premillennialists believe it is future:

Millennial View	Present		Future
Amillennialism	X		
Postmillennialism	X	or	X[3]
Premillennialism			X

An Explanation of the Views

I. View 1: Satan Is Presently Bound

According to amillennialists and many postmillennialists, the binding of Satan is a present reality because he was bound by Christ during His first-century ministry on earth.

A. The Timing of the Binding

According to this view, because several New Testament passages link the binding of Satan to the ministry of Christ in the first century, the binding of Revelation 20 must have taken place at that time. In other words, Satan is currently bound.

1. Matthew 12:29: "Or how can anyone enter the strong man's house and carry off his property, unless he first binds the strong man? And then he will plunder his house" (see Mark 3:27).

    According to Hamilton, "The context makes it perfectly plain that Christ was claiming that he could cast out demons because he had first bound Satan!" (Hamilton 1995: 131)

2. Luke 10:17-18: "And the seventy returned with joy, saying, 'Lord, even the demons are subject to us in Your name.' And He said to them, 'I was watching Satan fall from heaven like lightning.'"

    In the words of Hoekema, "Satan's kingdom had just been dealt a crushing blow—...a certain binding of Satan, a certain restriction of his power, had just taken place" (Hoekema 1979: 229).

3. John 12:31-32: "Now judgment is upon this world; now the ruler of this world shall be cast out. And I, if I be lifted up from the earth, will draw all men to Myself."

4. Colossians 2:15: "When He had disarmed the rulers and authorities, He made a public display of them, having triumphed over them through Him."

5. Hebrews 2:14-15: "Since then the children share in flesh and blood, He Himself likewise also partook of the same, that through death He might render powerless him who had the power of death, that is, the devil; and might deliver those who through fear of death were subject to slavery all their lives."

6. 1 John 3:8b: "The Son of God appeared for this purpose, that He might destroy the works of the devil."

7. Revelation 12:9: "And the great dragon was thrown down, the serpent of old who is called the devil and Satan, who deceives the whole world; he was thrown down to the earth, and his angels were thrown down with him."

B. The Nature of the Binding

Those who affirm the binding of Satan in Revelation 20 as a present reality do not believe that this binding *eliminated* Satan's activities on earth, but merely *limited* them to some extent. This is usually described as the *limiting*, the *curtailing*, the *curbing*, the *suppressing*, the *partial paralyzing*, the *restricting*, or the *restraining* of Satan's power and influence on earth, but again, not the *elimination* of it.

According to Cox, "Satan, though bound, still goes about like a roaring lion seeking whom he may devour. The chain with which he is bound is a long one, allowing him much freedom of movement" (Cox 1966: 139).

C. The Purpose of the Binding

Those who affirm the binding of Satan as a present reality point out that the devil is said to have been bound in Revelation 20 in *one* respect and one respect *only:* "so that he should not deceive the nations any longer" (v. 3b).

1. This is said to mean that Satan is unable to prevent the spread of the gospel to the nations of the world. In other words, because Satan is bound, he is unable to destroy the church as a missionary institution (see Rev 20:7-8, where Satan's release results in his resumed effort to destroy the church) and therefore unable to prevent the extension of the church throughout the world.

2. In the Old Testament era, the nations were in darkness, but the redemptive work of Christ and the binding of Satan "paved the way for successful proclamation of the gospel throughout the world" (Hamstra 1998: 120).[4]

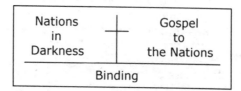

Nations in Darkness	Gospel to the Nations
Binding	

II. View 2: The Binding of Satan Is Yet Future

The second view is very simple. According to premillennialists, the binding of Satan in Revelation 20:1-3—and the thousand-year period during which Satan is bound—is yet future and will follow the Second Coming of Christ. During this time, Satan's activities and influence on earth will be completely eliminated.

An Evaluation of the Views

In examining evidence for the two views, five compelling reasons emerge for rejecting the binding of Satan as a present reality and for affirming that this confinement of the devil has yet to occur. These reasons are the present-day activity of Satan, the present-day deception by Satan, the stated purpose of the binding, the non-progressive nature of the binding, and the supposed parallels of the binding.

I. The Present-Day Activity of Satan

The binding of Satan in Revelation 20 indicates that the devil will be completely inactive on the earth during the thousand-year period, but the testimony of the New Testament indicates that Satan is quite active on the earth in the present age.

A. The Inactivity of Satan during the Thousand Years

1. Revelation 20 begins with an unnamed angel coming down from heaven with the key to the abyss and a great chain (v. 1). After laying hold of Satan, the angel binds him with the chain and

throws him into the abyss, shutting and sealing
the abyss over him (vv. 2-3a).[5]

a.   "The imagery of throwing Satan into a pit and
shutting it and sealing it over him gives a picture of total removal from influence on earth"
(Grudem 1994: 1117).

b.   "The elaborate measures taken to insure his
custody are most easily understood as imply-
ing the complete cessation of his influence on
earth (rather than a curbing of his activities)"
(Mounce 1977: 353).

c.   "If a symbolic presentation of the binding of
Satan were intended to teach that Satan was
rendered completely inactive, what more
dramatic picture could be provided than is
here portrayed?" (Walvoord 1986: 231).

2.   The fact that Satan is incarcerated and sealed in
the *abyss*—a prison for evil spirits[6]—is what most
clearly indicates the complete cessation of his activity and influence on earth during the thousand
years.

3.   The references to the abyss (*abussos*) in Luke
8:31 and Revelation 9, in particular, indicate that
confinement to the abyss entails the complete
removal of activity and influence upon the earth.

a.   In Luke 8:31, the demons possessing a man
entreat Jesus not to command them to depart
into the abyss, because they know that if he
does, they will no longer be free to wreak
havoc on the earth. Seeing a herd of swine
feeding on the mountain, the demons request
permission to enter them (v. 32). Jesus then
grants them permission, and so they depart
from the man to enter the swine, which they
proceed to drive into the lake where the swine
drown (vv. 32-33).

Confinement to the abyss would have prevented the demons' activity and influence on the

earth, but departure into the swine allowed them to roam free and continue to wreak havoc on the earth.[7]

b. In Revelation 9, "John sees a swarm of locusts [which are demons] coming up out of the pit. The harm caused by these pit locusts occurs only after they are released. The necessary implication is that their influence is not experienced by anyone as long as they are locked up in the pit. The graphic language about the key, opening the pit, subsequent instructions about harming, and coming on the earth...all converges to make the point that these 'locusts' had *no* influence on earthly inhabitants prior to the time of their release" (Blaising 1999: 217-18).

c. This can also be seen in Revelation 11:7 and 20:7-8. In 11:7 the beast must first *depart* from the abyss before he is able to make war with the two witnesses on earth, and when Satan is released from the abyss in 20:7-8, the text says that "he will *come out* to deceive the nations which are in the four corners of the *earth*" (v. 8; emphasis added).

But What About the Purpose Clause in Revelation 20:3?

Many amillennialists and postmillennialists respond by saying that the text itself says that Satan is bound in *one* respect and one respect *only:* "so that he should not deceive the nations any longer" (Rev 20:3). He is therefore free, they say, to partake in other activities here on earth.

The use of a purpose clause, however, does not preclude the possibility of other purposes or results of the action of the verb. To illustrate, "if a warden says that he is putting a prisoner in solitary confinement in order that he will no longer kill any more prisoners, this does not mean the prisoner is free to steal and do other such activities" (Powell 2001: 3). In the case of the binding of Satan in Revelation 20, then, the degree of Satan's restriction is determined not by the purpose clause but by the language of the text itself, which—as demonstrated above—indicates absolute confinement.[8]

    d. To be bound and confined in the abyss, then, is to be totally cut off from any activity or influence upon the earth.

B. The Activity of Satan in the Present Age

In contrast to this picture of Satan being bound and imprisoned in the abyss during the thousand years, the New Testament testifies repeatedly that Satan is extremely active on earth during the present age.

1. He entered Judas and influenced him to betray Christ (Luke 22:3; John 13:27).

2. He sought to sift Peter like wheat (Luke 22:31).

3. He filled the heart of Ananias and influenced him to lie to the Holy Spirit (Acts 5:3).

4. He sent a messenger to buffet the Apostle Paul (2 Cor 12:7).

5. He thwarted Paul from traveling to Thessalonica (1 Thess 2:18).

6. He snatches the Word of God from unbelieving hearers of the gospel before it can take root (Matt 13:19; Luke 8:12).

7. He tells lies (John 8:44).

8. He has unbelievers under his dominion (Acts 26:18).

9. He tempts believers (1 Cor 7:5).

10. He seeks to take advantage of believers (2 Cor 2:11).

11. He is called the "god of this world" (2 Cor 4:4).

12. He blinds the minds of the unbelieving (2 Cor 4:4).

13. He seeks to deceive believers as he did with Eve (2 Cor 11:3).

14. He disguises himself as an angel of light (2 Cor 11:14).

15. He is at work in unbelievers to influence them to live as they do (Eph 2:2).

16. He seeks to deceive believers as he battles against them (Eph 6:11-12).

17. He deceives and traps unbelievers (2 Tim 2:26).

18. He holds unbelievers captive to do his will (2 Tim 2:26).

19. He prowls about like a roaring lion, seeking someone to devour (1 Pet 5:8).

20. He is the father of those who practice sin (1 John 3:8-10).

21. He holds unbelievers in his power (1 John 5:19).

22. He is called the one who deceives the whole world (Rev 12:9).

23. He will deceive those who dwell upon the earth (Rev 13:14; 18:23; 19:20).

"If one accepts these Scriptures as testifying to the fact that Satan has power to tempt, to deceive, to blind, to buffet, to hinder, to work signs and lying wonders, and who is free like a raging lion to walk about seeking whom he may devour, how then can one hold that Satan is now bound?" (Walvoord 1959: 294). As Feinberg notes, "One cannot have Satan bound and loose at the same time; the logic of language will not permit it" (Feinberg 1980: 331).

The Bottom Line

Because the devil is active and influential on earth in the present age, the binding and incarceration of Satan in Revelation 20 cannot be a present reality and must have reference to a period of time in the future.

II. The Present-Day Deception by Satan

    A. The New Testament teaches that Satan is presently active (and will continue to be active) in the work of deception from which the binding of Satan in Revelation 20 will keep him.

        1. 2 Corinthians 4:3-4: "And even if our gospel is veiled, it is veiled to those who are perishing, in whose case the god of this world has blinded the minds of the unbelieving, that they might not see the light of the gospel of the glory of Christ, who is the image of God."[9]

        2. 2 Timothy 2:26: "...and they may come to their senses and escape from the snare of the devil, having been held captive by him to do his will."[10]

        3. 2 Corinthians 11:3: "But I am afraid, lest as the serpent deceived Eve by his craftiness, your minds should be led astray from the simplicity and purity of devotion to Christ."[11]

        4. Revelation 12:9: "And the great dragon was thrown down, the serpent of old who is called the devil and Satan, who deceives the whole world; he was thrown down to the earth, and his angels were thrown down with him."

        5. Revelation 13:14: "And he deceives those who dwell on the earth because of the signs which it was given him to perform in the presence of the beast, telling those who dwell on the earth to make an image to the beast who had the wound of the sword and has come to life."

        6. Revelation 16:13-16: "And I saw coming out of the mouth of the dragon and out of the mouth of the beast and out of the mouth of the false prophet, three unclean spirits like frogs; for they are spirits of demons, performing signs, which go out to the kings of the whole world, to gather them together for the war of the great day of God, the Almighty. ('Behold, I am coming like a thief. Blessed is the one who stays awake and keeps his

garments, lest he walk about naked and men see his shame.') And they gathered them together to the place which in Hebrew is called Har-Magedon."

B. Some who believe that Satan is currently bound have tried to alleviate the tension between their view and the New Testament teaching regarding Satan's present-day activity of deception.

1. For example, Garlington states that Revelation 20:2-3 does not imply "that Satan no longer engages in deceptive work" (Garlington 1997: 72).

    a. The problem with this statement is that it denies precisely that which Revelation 20:3 affirms.

    b. Garlington insists that Satan remains able to engage in works of deception, and Revelation 20:3 asserts that Satan is no longer able to deceive.

2. In similar fashion, Hendriksen asserts that the binding is simply a matter of degree: "If during the present N.T. era the devil 'blinds the minds of unbelievers,' II Cor. 4:4, that was true even *more emphatically* during the old dispensation" (Hendriksen 1967: 224; emphasis added).[12]

    a. The difficulty with this explanation is that Revelation 20:2-3 teaches not that Satan's ability to deceive was *limited*, but rather that it was *eliminated*.

    b. In other words, the text does not say that Satan will deceive the nations *less* than he did in the past—it says that he will deceive the nations *no longer*.

C. Satan's present-day work of deception, then, proves that he is not currently bound and incarcerated as described in Revelation 20:1-3.[13]

III. The Stated Purpose of the Binding

    A. Those who believe Satan is presently bound generally teach that the purpose (and therefore result) of Satan's binding is that he is now unable to prevent the spread of the gospel to the nations of the world (Rev 20:3).

        1. The idea is that although the nations lived in darkness in the Old Testament era, Christ came to earth two thousand years ago and bound Satan.

        2. Therefore, Satan was no longer able to prevent the evangelization of the world, and the age of world missions had begun.

    B. The difficulty with this view is that the purpose clause in Revelation 20:3 does not say that the binding of Satan keeps him from preventing the missionary activity of the church to the nations.

        1. In fact, this clause concerns itself not at all with the freedom of believers to *proclaim* the truth, but rather with the ability of unbelievers to *perceive* the truth.

        2. Therefore, there is no indication in Revelation 20:1-3 that the primary purpose of Satan's binding was to allow the gospel to go forth to Gentile nations that had been previously deprived of the Good News.

IV. The Non-Progressive Nature of the Binding

Amillennialists and postmillennialists usually assert that the binding of Satan has a progressive nature to it, but this is not supported by Revelation 20:1-3.

    A. Amillennialism generally teaches that the binding of Satan did not take place at a specific point in time, but rather that the binding *began* when Jesus resisted Satan's temptations in the wilderness, continued during His earthly ministry, and was culminated at the time of His death and resurrection.

1. This raises the question of when exactly it was that Satan was bound and thrown into the abyss by the angel in Revelation 20:

   a. In Matthew 4 when Jesus resisted Satan's temptations?

   b. In Matthew 12 when Jesus bound the strong man?

   c. Or in Matthew 27 and 28 when Jesus died and was resurrected?

2. The problem is that the picture painted in Revelation 20 is not one of Satan being bound over a period of time (either through a process or as a series of individual bindings), but rather one of him being bound at a specific point in time at the beginning of the thousand years.

B. Postmillennialism generally teaches that the binding of Satan is a process that continues throughout the current church age "as evil is more and more suppressed" and "the world is more and more Christianized" (Boettner 1957: 127). In other words, Satan is bound progressively and therefore his deceptive power over the nations gradually fades as the kingdom of Christ grows through the advance of the gospel into the world.

1. However, as Blaising notes, "There is nothing in Revelation 20:1-3 that supports the idea that the binding is an 'increasing' phenemon, taking place throughout the age" (Blaising 1999: 80).

2. Put simply, the postmillennial view of Christ's visible kingdom being established gradually appears nowhere in the passage itself.

C. Premillennialism's teaching that the binding of Satan takes place at one specific point in time—in a non-progressive manner—is most naturally supported by Revelation 20:1-3.

V. The Supposed Parallels of the Binding

Those who understand the binding of Satan as a present reality almost always link Revelation 20:1-3 with various texts in the New Testament in order to connect the binding to the ministry of Christ in the first century. An examination of these texts, however, demonstrates that these supposed parallels do not support the position that Satan is currently bound as recorded in Revelation 20.

A. Matthew 4:1-11 and Luke 4:1-13

1. Some believe that Christ's work of binding Satan began when the Lord triumphed over him by resisting his temptations in the wilderness.

2. The text, however, indicates that Satan left the scene defeated but unbound, which is confirmed by Luke's notation that the devil departed "until an opportune time" (Luke 4:13). There is no indication of any kind of binding in Matthew 4 and Luke 4.

B. Matthew 12:29

1. In Matthew 12:29, Jesus is continuing His response to the accusation that He is casting out demons by the power of Satan. He has already shown that He is Satan's *enemy* (vv. 25-28), and now He shows that He is also Satan's *master:* "Or how can anyone enter the strong man's house and carry off his property, unless he first binds the strong man? And then he will plunder his house" (v. 29).

   a. With this parable, Jesus explains that the very exorcism for which He was condemned is a demonstration of His sovereignty over Satan and his forces. For how else could Jesus have plundered the strong man's house (i.e., robbed Satan of his spiritual property by delivering the demoniac) unless he had first bound the strong man (i.e., rendered him powerless to prevent the exorcism)?

b. In performing the exorcism, then, Jesus was not casting out the demons by Satan's power—He was demonstrating His own power over Satan.[14]

2. Although some equate Matthew 12:29 with the binding of Satan in Revelation 20:1-3, the two passages have more differences than similarities.[15]

   a. In Revelation 20:1-3 an angel imprisons Satan and he is prevented from deceiving the nations, but in Matthew 12:29 Christ himself binds Satan, and Satan is unable to keep Christ from exercising his authority over demons (Powell 2001: 4).

   b. "The binding of Satan [in Matt 12] does not restrict all of Satan's activities, but simply demonstrates that Jesus is sovereign over him and his demonic forces" (ibid.: 3).

3. While the binding in Revelation 20 leaves Satan imprisoned in the abyss and renders him unable to deceive the nations or exercise any other kind of influence upon the earth, the binding in Matthew 12 leaves Satan prowling about the earth and yet unable to maintain control of an individual through his demons when Christ determines to deliver that individual.[16]

4. There is, then, a lack of evidence to equate the bindings of Satan in Matthew 12 and Revelation 20.[17]

C. Luke 10:17-18

1. In Luke 10, the seventy whom Jesus had sent out return to Him saying, "Lord, even the demons are subject to us in Your name" (v. 17).

2. Then Jesus says to them in response, "I was watching Satan fall from heaven like lightning" (v. 18).

3. In His statement, Jesus is most likely looking forward to the ultimate defeat of Satan that would be secured at the cross and executed fully when Satan is thrown into the lake of fire.

   a. As Green notes, "The decisive fall of Satan is anticipated in the future, but it is already becoming manifest through the mission of Jesus and, by extension, through the ministry of his envoys" (Green 1997: 419).

   b. In this way, the success of the seventy was viewed by Jesus "as a symbol and earnest" of the complete and future overthrow of Satan (Plummer 1975: 278).

4. The pivotal question here is this: Does Jesus' statement about Satan falling like lightning require that the events described in Revelation 20:1-3 be placed in a time period beginning with the earthly ministry of Christ and extending into the present?

   a. The simple answer is that it does not.

   b. In looking toward the ultimate destruction of the devil, Jesus in no way described Satan as being presently bound and imprisoned in the abyss, unable to deceive the nations.

5. While the success of the seventy demonstrates the authority of Christ over the demons and points forward to the ultimate destruction of Satan, there is no indication in this text that the events of Revelation 20:1-3 are being described or referred to as a current reality.[18]

D. John 12:31, Colossians 2:15, Hebrews 2:14-15, and 1 John 3:8

1. These verses all refer to Christ's victory at the cross in which He triumphed over Satan and delivered from his control those who repent and believe in the Savior.

2. The view that equates this victory with the action taken against Satan in Revelation 20:1-3a cannot account for the release of Satan in Revelation 20:3b and 7, for whatever is accomplished in the binding of verse 3 is undone in the release of verse 7.

   a. "These words are difficult to understand if they are applied to our Lord's binding of Satan in his earthly ministry. The victory he won over Satan [on the cross] was won once and for all. Satan will never be loosed from bondage to Christ won by his death and resurrection" (Ladd 1972: 263).

   b. As Thomas asks, "What restrictions currently placed on him will be removed at the end of this age" (Thomas 1995: 404)?

E. Revelation 12:9

   1. Although some claim that Revelation 12:9 and Revelation 20:1-3 are parallel to one another, the details of the two passages demonstrate that they are not.

      a. In Revelation 12:9, Satan is removed from heaven by Michael and his angels and thrown down to the earth where he will proceed to deceive the whole world for a short time.

      b. In Revelation 20:1-3, Satan is removed from the earth by an angel and thrown into the abyss from which he will be unable to deceive the whole world for a thousand years.

   2. The complete lack of agreement in the details of these two passages clearly shows that they are speaking of two different events that happen at two different times:

Revelation 12:9	Revelation 20:1-3
removed from *heaven*	removed from *earth*
removed by Michael and his angels	removed by *one* angel
thrown down to the *earth*	thrown into the *abyss*
deceiving the world	*unable* to deceive the world
a short time	a thousand years

3. Revelation 12:9 and 20:1-3, then, are not parallel to one another, and the former adds no support to the view that the binding of Satan in the latter is a present reality.

Conclusion

Hundreds of years before the first coming of Christ, Satan was found to be "roaming about on the earth and walking around on it" (Job 1:7), and today—hundreds of years *after* the first coming—Satan still "prowls about like a roaring lion, seeking someone to devour" (1 Pet 5:8). Simply stated, Satan is not currently bound and imprisoned in the abyss, and the millennium of Revelation 20 has not yet begun.

Chapter 4
The Nature of the First Resurrection: Spiritual or Physical?

The Significance of the Question

The question concerning the "first resurrection" of Revelation 20:4-6 is whether it is a *spiritual* resurrection or a *physical* resurrection. If this resurrection is *physical*, the thousand-year period of Revelation 20 must be *future*—the position of pre-millennialism—for such a resurrection has not yet taken place. If, however, this resurrection is spiritual, the thousand-year period may be taking place in the present—the position of amillennialism and postmillennialism.

Millennial View	Spiritual	Physical
Amillennialism	X	
Postmillennialism	X[19]	
Premillennialism		X

An Evaluation of the Views

While the consensus is that the "first resurrection" of verse 5 refers back to "they came to life" in verse 4, three views have arisen regarding the precise nature of this resurrection. The first two views hold to a spiritual resurrection, while the third affirms a physical resurrection.

I. View 1: The Spiritual Resurrection of Regeneration

    A. The Explanation of View 1

        1. In this view, the "first resurrection" refers to the regeneration of the believer at the point of conversion. In this way, the first resurrection is understood as the "initiation into the Christian life in the present age" (Page 1980: 37).

        2. "We believe entrance into the on-going millennium is gained solely through the new birth, and that John refers to this as the first resurrection" (Cox 1966: 4).

        3. "This first resurrection is—salvation" (Gentry 1998: 85).

    B. The Support for View 1

        1. Throughout the New Testament, the new birth is depicted as *a rising from the dead* (i.e., a "resurrection").

            a. Mark 12:26-27: "But regarding the fact that the dead rise again, have you not read in the book of Moses, in the passage about the burning bush, how God spoke to him, saying, 'I am the God of Abraham, and the God of Isaac, and the God of Jacob'? He is not the God of the dead, but of the living; you are greatly mistaken."

            b. John 5:25-29: "Truly, truly, I say to you, an hour is coming and now is, when the dead shall hear the voice of the Son of God; and those who hear shall live. For just as the Father has life in Himself, even so He gave to the Son also to have life in Himself; and He gave Him authority to execute judgment, because He is the Son of Man. Do not marvel at this; for an hour is coming, in which all who are in the tombs shall hear His voice, and shall come forth; those who did the good deeds to a resurrection of life, those who committed the evil deeds to a resurrection of judgment."

c. John 11:25: "Jesus said to her, 'I am the resurrection and the life; he who believes in Me shall live even if he dies....'"

d. Romans 6:4-6: "Therefore we have been buried with Him through baptism into death, in order that as Christ was raised from the dead through the glory of the Father, so we too might walk in newness of life. For if we have become united with Him in the likeness of His death, certainly we shall be also in the likeness of His resurrection, knowing this, that our old self was crucified with Him, that our body of sin might be done away with, that we should no longer be slaves to sin."

e. Romans 8:10-11: "And if Christ is in you, though the body is dead because of sin, yet the spirit is alive because of righteousness. But if the Spirit of Him who raised Jesus from the dead dwells in you, He who raised Christ Jesus from the dead will also give life to your mortal bodies through His Spirit who indwells you."

f. Ephesians 2:1, 4-6: "And you were dead in your trespasses and sin....But God, being rich in mercy, because of His great love with which He loved us, even when we were dead in our transgressions, made us alive together with Christ (by grace you have been saved), and raised us up with Him, and seated us with Him in the heavenly places, in Christ Jesus...."

g. Colossians 2:12-13: "...having been buried with Him in baptism, in which you were also raised up with Him through faith in the working of God, who raised Him from the dead. And when you were dead in your transgressions and the uncircumcision of your flesh, He made you alive together with Him, having forgiven us all our transgressions...."

h. Colossians 3:1: "If then you have been raised up with Christ, keep seeking the things above, where Christ is, seated at the right hand of God."

i. 1 John 3:14: "We know that we have passed out of death into life, because we love the brethren."[20]

j. 1 John 5:11-13: "And the witness is this, that God has given us eternal life, and this life is in His Son. He who has the Son has the life; he who does not have the Son of God does not have the life. These things I have written to you who believe in the name of the Son of God, in order that you may know that you have eternal life."

This constant use of resurrection terminology to refer to the new birth is said to provide clear evidence that the first resurrection of Revelation 20:4-5 is spiritual regeneration.

2. Because the subjects of this resurrection are "souls" (*psuchas*) in verse 4, the first resurrection must refer to spiritual regeneration.

According to Hamilton, "The deliberate choice of the word 'soul,' which almost universally means soul as distinct from body, as applying to the believers now reigning with Christ in glory, seems to make it perfectly plain that the first resurrection is [the new birth]. If it were a literal resurrection of the body, why should the author choose a word which almost always does *not* mean body?" (Hamilton 1955: 134).

C. The Refutation of View 1

Despite the arguments in favor of the view that the first resurrection refers to regeneration, there are four difficulties with this interpretation that preclude it as a possibility.

1. This view requires a use of the word "resurrection" (*anastasis*) that is unprecedented in the New Testament.

   a. Of the 42 times that it is used in the New Testament, the word "resurrection" is never used to refer to regeneration.

   b. In light of this, it is unlikely that the "first resurrection" refers to the new birth.[21]

2. This view requires that the word *ezesan* in verse 4 (the aorist tense of *zao*, "to live") be understood in a completely different sense than the *ezesan* in verse 5.

   a. "If [*ezesan*] in vs. 4 designates spiritual life at conversion...we are faced with the problem of the same word being used in the same context with two entirely different meanings, with no indication whatsoever as to the change of meaning" (Ladd 1972: 265-66).

   b. "Because both the first and second resurrections are described in identical terminology, *ezesan*, and because no qualifying adjectives or adverbs or anything else indicate that the two resurrections are different in kind, the attempt to make them different appears to be purely arbitrary" (Erickson 1998: 99).

3. The grammar of the passage indicates that the entire group of saints begins its reign together and continues this reign for the entire 1000-year period.[22]

   a. This proposes a significant problem, for the interpretation of view 1 has individuals entering their reign with Christ at the time of their conversion some time after the 1000-year period has begun.

   b. In addition, view 1 also teaches that the entrance of the saints into their reign is distributed throughout the millennial period, some not being converted and entering into it until the period is almost over (Powell 2001: 10). This stands in contrast to the picture of Revelation 20 in which the entire group of saints begins its reign together.

4. According to this view, the individuals described in verse 4 are not regenerated by the Holy Spirit until *after* they are martyred for their faith in Christ.

   a. "If this verse refers to the new birth, then the martyrs were beheaded before they were born again" (MacLeod, 2000: 57).

   b. This interpretation introduces "the absurdity of having souls being regenerated after they had been beheaded for their faithfulness to Christ!" (McClain 1974: 488).

II. View 2: The Spiritual Resurrection of the Soul's Ascension

   A. The Explanation of View 2

      1. In this interpretation, the first resurrection refers to "the translation of the soul from this sinful earth to God's holy heaven" at the point of physical death (Hendriksen 1967: 231-32).

      2. In other words, when the believer dies physically, his soul is raised and ascends from earth to heaven, "the effect of which is the living and reigning with Christ a thousand years" (Hughes 1973: 290-91).

   B. The Support for View 2

      1. It seems to fit the context. The idea is that the believers are martyred and their souls are raised or translated to heaven where they live and reign with Christ.

      2. The verb "to live" (*zao*) is used at least twice to refer to the existence of souls after the death of the body.

    a. Luke 20:38: "Now He is not the God of the dead, but of the living; for all *live* to Him" (emphasis added).

    b. 1 Peter 4:6: "For the gospel has for this purpose been preached even to those who are dead, that though they are judged in the flesh as men, they may *live* in the spirit according to the will of God" (emphasis added).

C. The Refutation of View 2

  1. This understanding of the verb "to live" (*zao*) is not supported by the context.

    a. In all of its 139 appearances in the New Testament, only twice is *zao* used to refer to spiritual life after physical death (Luke 20:38 and 1 Pet 4:6), and in both of these uses the context makes it clear that it has reference to spiritual life.[23]

    b. No such clear contextual indicators can be found in Revelation 20.

  2. The word "resurrection" (*anastasis*) is never used in the New Testament to refer to the translation of the believer's soul into heaven at the point of death.

    As Feinberg points out, "When believers die, they can die in one realm only—the physical; when they come alive, they do so in one area only—the physical. Where does Scripture teach otherwise?" (Feinberg 1980: 335).

  3. This view erroneously denies the existence of a second resurrection at the end of the thousand years. In other words, when John says in verse 5 that "the rest of the dead did not come to life until the thousand years were completed," proponents of view 2 understand this to mean that the "rest of the dead" never do come to life.[24]

4. The grammar of the passage indicates that the entire group of saints begins its reign together and continues this reign for the entire 1000-year period.[25]

    a. This proposes a significant problem, for in the interpretation of view 2 the martyred saints enter into their reign with Christ upon their death some time after the 1000-year period has begun.

    b. In addition, view 2 teaches that the entrance of the martyred saints into their reign is distributed throughout the millennial period, some not entering into it until the period is almost over (Powell 2001: 10).[26] This stands in contrast to the picture of Revelation 20 in which the entire group of saints begins its reign together.

III. The Physical Resurrection of the Redeemed

A. The Explanation of View 3

1. In this view, the first resurrection refers to believers who will physically come to life at the beginning of the thousand years. The first resurrection will restore believers to bodily life for their millennial reign,[27] whereas the second resurrection will bring "the rest of the dead" (i.e., all unbelievers) before the great white throne to be judged (Rev 20:11-13).

2. "The sharp contrast in the passage is between those who are raised at the beginning of the thousand years and those who are raised at the end. Both are physical resurrections, but those who are raised at the beginning of the Millennium, designated as the 'first resurrection,' are contrasted to those who 'come to life' at the end of the Millennium, who face judgment according to Revelation 20:11-15" (Walvoord 1986: 236).

B. The Support for View 3

    1. The noun "resurrection" (*anastasis*) is used almost exclusively in the New Testament in reference to *physical* resurrection.

    2. The exact same form of the verb (*ezesan*, the aorist tense of *zao*) is used in verses 4 and 5, and in verse 5 it clearly refers to a bodily resurrection.

        a. It is most reasonable, then, to understand its use in verse 4 as a reference to bodily resurrection as well.

        b. These two uses of *ezesan* correspond to the "first resurrection" (in v. 5b) and the "second resurrection" (implied in v. 5a and implied by the very idea of a *first* resurrection).

    3. When the verb "to live" (*zao*) is used in the context of bodily death in the New Testament, it always speaks of bodily resurrection (Thomas 1995: 417; see John 11:25; Acts 1:3; 9:41).

        a. As McClain notes, "if the people involved were beheaded physically, and then lived again, common sense would suggest that they received back the same category of life that had been lost" (McClain 1974: 488).

        b. In similar fashion, Saucy notes that they are "portrayed as physically dead just before the statement 'They came to life and reigned' (v. 4), which suggests that this new life is physical" (Saucy 1993: 275).

C. The Defense of View 3

    1. Objection 1

        a. Articulated: "This interpretation contradicts Scripture's teaching of a general resurrection."

        As Gentry asks, "Why should we believe that the New Testament everywhere teaches a general, singular resurrection on the last day, only to discover later in the most difficult book of the Bible that there are actually two specific, distantly separated resurrections for different classes of people?" (Gentry 1999: 243).

    i.   John 5:28-29: "Do not marvel at this; for an hour is coming, in which all who are in the tombs shall hear His voice, and shall come forth; those who did the good deeds to a resurrection of life, those who committed the evil deeds to a resurrection of judgment."

    ii. Daniel 12:2: "And many of those who sleep in the dust of the ground will awake, these to everlasting life, but the others to disgrace and everlasting contempt."

    iii. Acts 24:15: "...there shall certainly be a resurrection of both the righteous and the wicked."

b. Considered: These passages do not exclude the idea of two resurrections—they simply do not specify whether or not the resurrection of the believers and unbelievers will be separated in time (Grudem 1994: 1119).

    i.   John 5:28-29 in fact speaks of two different resurrections—a resurrection of life and a resurrection of judgment—and the order of the two is even the same as in Revelation 20.[28]

    ii. Acts 24:15 affirms that both the righteous and the wicked will be raised from the dead, but it does not exclude the possibility that this would happen at different times.

    iii. Daniel 12:2 simply says that both types of people will be raised but does not specify whether the two groups of individuals will be raised simultaneously or at different times.

Therefore, while these passages do not specify the timing of the two resurrections, in Revelation 20:5 this time element *is* specified—one thousand years will separate the resurrection of the righteous and the resurrection of the wicked.[29]

2. Objection 2:

   a. Articulated: "Both verbs in verse 4 ("to live" and "to reign") are in the *aorist* tense."

   Because it is agreed that the second verb is to be construed as a *constative* aorist ("they reigned"), the first verb must also be construed as a constative ("they lived"), not an ingressive ("they came to life"). (A constative aorist views the action as a whole ["they lived"], while an ingressive aorist stresses the beginning of an action or entrance into a state of being ["they came to life"].) Therefore, rather than being translated "they came to life" (i.e., a resurrection), the verb should be translated "they lived" (i.e., lived in heaven after death, in keeping with view 2 of the resurrection).

   b. Considered: There is no rule of grammar that says that the first verb ("to live") cannot be ingressive while the second verb ("to reign") is constative. In fact, in this context the aorist is the most appropriate tense to express both the ingressive idea of "to live" (i.e., "they came to life") and the constative idea of "to reign" (i.e., "they reigned").[30]

3. Objection 3:

   a. Articulated: "The aorist tense of the verb 'to live' (*zao*) is rarely ingressive."

At least one amillennialist raises the objection that the aorist tense of the verb *zao* is used ingressively (i.e., "came to life") only twice in the entire New Testament (Rom 14:9 and Rev 2:8) (Hughes 1973: 290).

b. Considered: This objection carries no weight because the aorist tense of *zao* is used a total of only *eight* times in the entire New Testament.

    In addition, the aorist tense of *zao* in Luke 15:32 and Revelation 13:14 could also be considered ingressive, possibly bringing the total to four of its eight occurrences.

Conclusion

The "first resurrection" of Revelation 20:4-5 is best understood as a physical resurrection of the righteous. Because such a resurrection has not yet taken place, the thousand years described in Revelation 20 must refer to a period of time yet future, the view of premillennialism.

Chapter 5
The Duration of the Thousand Years: Symbolic or Literal?

The Significance of the Question

The question regarding the length of the millennium is this: Should the thousand years in Revelation 20 be understood literally as one thousand calendar years or symbolically as a figurative way to designate a period of some other length?

Amillennialists and postmillennialists teach that the thousand years should be taken symbolically, whereas most premillennialists—but not all—believe that the thousand years should be taken literally.[31]

Millennial View	Symbolic	Literal
Amillennialism	X	
Postmillennialism	X[32]	
Premillennialism		X

Because more than one thousand calendar years have transpired since the first coming of Christ, the question of the duration of the thousand years is significant: If the "thousand years" is literal, it cannot refer to the period of time separating the two advents of Christ (the position of amillennialism), and it therefore must have reference to a period of time yet future (the position of premillennialism).

The Symbolic View of the Duration

I.   The Explanation of the Symbolic View

    A.   Those who regard the "thousand years" to be symbolic explain the meaning of this symbol in various ways. They have described the thousand years as referring to or symbolizing:

        1.   "a long period of time"

        2.   "a great epoch in human history"

        3.   "an indefinitely long time"

        4.   "a vast, undefined period of time"

        5.   "a long period"

        6.   "an indefinite period"

        7.   "a complete period"

        8.   "a very long period of indeterminate length"

        9.   an "indefinite period of time"

      10.   "an ideal time"

      11.   "an extended, but indefinite, period of time"

      12.   "a long period of time, the exact extent of which is unknown"

      13.   "a complete period of time, the length of which is known only by God"

      14.   "an indefinitely long period of time"

      15.   "a complete, perfect number of years"

      16.   "a definitely limited period"

17. "the complete time that God has determined"

18. "completeness"

19. "a period of fullness"

20. a "great and full" period of time

B. Most of these explanations fall into one or both of these two categories:

   1. "an indefinitely long period of time"

   2. "a complete period of time determined and known only by God"

C. Regardless of the precise understanding of what the thousand years symbolizes, it is understood to refer to a period of time between the first and second comings of Christ.[33] In other words, the "thousand years" of Revelation 20 could actually be *thousands* of years.

II. The Support for the Symbolic View

There are two primary arguments for the symbolic view.

A. The book of Revelation is full of symbolism.

   1. "Since symbolism is used extensively throughout the Apocalypse and numbers are used in a non-literal sense frequently, it would be facile to insist that the number 'one thousand' be taken literally in this context" (Page 1980: 32).

   2. "Like the book as a whole, chapter 20 is highly symbolic. It speaks of Satan being bound with a chain and cast into a bottomless pit, and it anticipates a second death that lasts forever. The author obviously intended that none of these be interpreted in a purely literal manner, as such an interpretation would be nonsensical—that is, a spiritual being bound with a physical chain and confined in a physical pit with no bottom. Consequently, it is possible that other figures in these

verses, including the thousand years, are likewise to be understood symbolically" (Grenz 1992: 167).

3. "If the thousand years serve as a literal time frame, why is it only mentioned in one highly symbolic book?" (Gentry 1999: 51).

4. "We may readily assume that the number is symbolic, for numbers are used symbolically throughout Revelation" (Strimple 1999: 127).

B. The number one thousand is symbolically significant.

1. "Since the number ten signifies completeness, and since a thousand is ten to the third power, we may think of the expression 'a thousand years' as standing for a complete period, a very long period of indeterminate length" (Hoekema 1979: 227).

2. "The sacred number seven in combination with the equally sacred number three forms the number of holy perfection, then, and when this ten is cubed into a thousand, the seer has said all he could say to convey to our minds the idea of absolute completeness" (Warfield 1929: 654).

3. According to Chilton, the number ten "contains the idea of fullness of quantity" and stands for "many-ness," and when it is cubed, it expresses "great vastness" (Chilton 1987: 506).

4. Gentry states that "ten is the number of quantitative perfection (apparently because it is the full complement of digits on a person's hands or feet)" (Gentry 1999: 52). Furthermore, because one thousand is the cube of ten, it is "surely a symbolic sum representing quantitative perfection" (Gentry 1998: 82).

III. The Problems with the Symbolic View

There are six problems with the symbolic view, the last two being the most significant.

A. The appeal to the symbolic nature of the book of Revelation is overly simplistic.

 1. Because there is much in Revelation that is *not* symbolic, the presence of symbolism in the book hardly establishes the symbolic interpretation of the thousand years as the correct one.

 2. "The recognition of the symbolic language of the Apocalypse does not carry with it the corollary that every phrase must involve a symbol" (Ladd 1952: 148).

 3. Because not everything in Revelation is symbolic, one must provide compelling reasons why something should be considered symbolic.

B. The abundance of symbolic numbers in the book of Revelation has been exaggerated.

 1. In fact, some have argued that "no number in Revelation is verifiably a symbolic number" (Thomas 1995: 408) and that "there is no solid evidence that any of the numbers of the Revelation referring to time periods are other than literal" (Walvoord 1966: 288).

 2. To simply state that the thousand years of Revelation 20 should be understood symbolically because the book is "full of symbolic numbers" will not suffice. As Townsend notes, the approach of the interpreter must be to "look for clues in the biblical text which indicate whether a term is used literally or figuratively" (Townsend 1983: 213).

 3. In other words, one must take the phrases and numbers on a case-by-case basis when seeking to determine whether a literal or symbolic meaning is intended.[34]

C. There seems to be no precedent in Scripture for a non-literal use of the designation "thousand years."[35]

 1. Outside of Revelation 20, the designation occurs only in Psalm 90:4 and 2 Peter 3:8.

2. The meaning of the statements made in these two verses is dependent on the literal meaning of "thousand years."[36]

D. John's specific time designation of "a thousand years" stands in contrast to his use of the indefinite phrase "a short time" in verse 3.

   1. Had John intended to communicate the idea of a long period of time, wouldn't it be expected that he would use the phrase "a long time" in the same way that he referred to "a short time" in the same context?[37]

   2. As Feinberg notes, the Greek language knows well how to express "after a long time" (e.g., *polun chronon* in Matt 25:19) (Feinberg 1980: 333).

E. The duration of the binding was not *seen* by John in the vision—it was *directly revealed* to him by the Holy Spirit.

   1. As Walvoord writes, "Although the symbolic is obviously subject to interpretation, when God directs a prophet to record the meaning of what he saw, what is recorded is not symbolic but literal" (Walvoord 1986: 232).

   2. Thus, because the duration of the binding "was not part of the symbolic revelation but a direct communication from God to John," it should be taken literally (ibid.).

F. The phrase "thousand years" in Revelation 20 possesses neither of the two characteristics of symbolic language.

   In order to be considered symbolic, the language in question must possess (a) some degree of *absurdity* when taken literally and (b) some degree of *clarity* when taken symbolically.[38]

1. The Absurdity of the Literal Interpretation

    a. The literal meaning of symbolic language causes the interpreter to scratch his head and ask, "But how can this be?"

    b. For example, when the reader of Isaiah 55:12 comes to the symbolic clause "the trees of the field will clap their hands," the literal meaning of these words possesses a degree of absurdity and causes him to ask, "But how is it that trees can clap their hands?"[39]

    c. With symbolic language, then, there is something inherent in the language itself that compels the interpreter to seek something other than a literal meaning: "Since trees don't *have* hands and therefore cannot *clap* their hands," he rightly reasons, "there must be a symbolic meaning to this clause."

2. The Clarity of the Symbolic Interpretation

    a. Symbolic language effectively communicates what it symbolizes. In other words, when the interpreter has concluded that the literal meaning of the language is absurd and ought to be abandoned, the symbolic interpretation will yield some degree of clarity to the meaning of the language of the text.

    b. For example, the symbolic language of the aforementioned clause in Isaiah 55:12 ("the trees...will clap their hands") clearly and effectively communicates that Israel's return from exile will be a time of great rejoicing.

    c. With symbolic language, then, the meaning intended by the symbolism is essentially clear and understandable.[40]

With this in mind, it is difficult to imagine why one would consider the "thousand years" in Revelation 20 to be symbolic language, for it possesses neither a degree of absurdity when taken literally, nor a degree of clarity when taken symbolically:

The Absurdity of the Literal Interpretation?

When the interpreter comes to Revelation 20 and encounters the "thousand years," nothing about this designation in its context compels him to seek a meaning other than the literal. Nothing compels him to scratch his head and ask, "But how can this be?"[41] Simply stated, there is nothing even slightly absurd or nonsensical about the literal meaning of the six uses of "thousand years" in Revelation 20.[42]

The Clarity of the Symbolic Interpretation?

At the same time, the designation "thousand years" also fails to effectively communicate any clear meaning when taken as a symbol. The explanations offered by those who take the "thousand years" figuratively are less than convincing and far less than clear.[43]

Conclusion

The best approach is to assume that all numbers "should always be taken at face value and understood as conveying a mathematical quantity unless there is either textual or contextual evidence to the contrary" (Davis 1941: 715-16). In the absence of such evidence, it is best to affirm the literal meaning of "thousand years" in Revelation and therefore reject the interpretation that sees this time period extending from the first coming to Christ to His Second Coming.[44]

Chapter 6
The Millennial Reign of Jesus Christ

Introduction

Because Revelation 20:4-6 speaks of believers who reign with Christ for a thousand years, these verses are often said to set forth what is called the "millennial reign" of Christ. There are four significant aspects of the nature of Christ's millennial reign—its locale, its basis, its participants, and its primary features:

Four Key Questions:

1. Where does this reign take place?
2. What is the basis of this reign?
3. Who will participate in this reign?
4. What are the primary features of this reign?

The Nature of the Millennial Reign

I.   The Locale of the Millennial Reign

    A.   An Explanation of the Millennial Positions

        The question to be considered here is whether the reign of Christ and the saints takes place in heaven or on earth. The three millennial views present three different answers to this question.

1. Amillennialism

    The millennial reign of Christ takes place in heaven, not on earth.[45]

    a. According to Hoekema, "whereas the thousand-year period described in these six verses is the same throughout, verses 1-3 describe what happens on earth during this time, and verses 4-6 depict what happens in heaven" (Hoekema 1979: 230).

    b. In the view of amillennialism, therefore, the thousand years of Revelation 20:1-6 refers to the present reign of Christ and the saints in heaven.

2. Postmillennialism

    The millennial reign of Christ takes place both in heaven *and* on earth.

    a. "Does this reign of the saints take place in heaven or on earth? The answer should be obvious: both! The saints' thrones are in heaven, with Christ (Eph. 2:6); yet, with their Lord, they exercise rule and dominion on earth (cf. 2:26-27; 5:10; 11:15)" (Chilton 1987: 514).

    b. In other words, Christ reigns from heaven, but He exercises His dominion through the saints here on earth.

3. Premillennialism

    The millennial reign of Christ will take place upon the earth as Jesus reigns from the Davidic throne in Jerusalem.

The difference between the three views, then, can be charted like this:

Millennial View	Heaven		Earth
Amillennialism	X		
Postmillennialism	X	and	X
Premillennialism			X

To further distinguish between the three positions on the millennial reign of Christ, it is helpful to consider the question, "Where is Christ during this reign—in heaven or on earth?" Amillennialism and postmillennialism say heaven, but premillennialism says earth.

Where Is Christ During the Millennium?		
Millennial View	**Heaven**	**Earth**
Amillennialism	X	
Postmillennialism	X	
Premillennialism		X

B. The Case for an Earthly Reign

In contrast to the claim of those who say there is "no indication in these verses that John is describing an earthly millennial reign" (Hoekema 1979: 235), there are at least five reasons to believe that the millennial reign will take place here on earth and not in heaven.

1. Revelation 5:10 identifies the location of the saints' reign to be "upon the earth."

2. When the seventh trumpet sounds in Revelation 11:15, heavenly voices proclaim, "The kingdom of the *world* has become the kingdom of our Lord, and of His Christ, and He will reign forever and ever" (emphasis added).

3. The elimination of Satan's activities and influence on *earth* is part of what makes the millennial reign possible (the binding of Satan is unnecessary for a millennial reign that takes place in heaven).

4. Revelation 20:9 indicates that the saints who reign for a thousand years are living "on the broad plain of the earth."

5. Revelation teaches that Christ will return to *earth* to defeat the nations (19:11-16), after which He will reign for a thousand years (20:4-6).[46]

II. The Basis of the Millennial Kingdom

Interestingly, Revelation 20:4-6 says little about the basis of the millennial kingdom. However, because the nature of the millennium is the subject of so much Old Testament prophecy, it is assumed that the reader knows and understands this basis from earlier revelation.

A proper understanding of this earlier revelation leads to the conclusion that the millennial kingdom of Revelation 20 finds its roots in the covenants of promise in the Old Testament—the Abrahamic Covenant, the Davidic Covenant, and the New Covenant.

A. The Abrahamic Covenant (Gen 12:1-3, 7; 15:7-21; 17:1-21)

In His covenant with Abraham, Yahweh promised (a) to bless Abraham, (b) to make Abraham's name great, (c) to make him a great nation, (d) to grant to him and his descendants the land of Canaan as an everlasting possession,[47] and (e) to bless the nations through him.

B. The Davidic Covenant (2 Sam 7:8-16; 1 Chron 17:7-15)[48]

In His covenant with David, Yahweh promised (a) to make David's name great, (b) to plant Israel in the land of Canaan and preserve her there in peace and security, (c) to preserve the line of David's descendants, and (d) to establish one of David's descendants as king over His kingdom forever.

C. The New Covenant (Jer 31:31-34; Ezek 36:24-38; Rom 11:26-27)

In the New Covenant, Yahweh promised to the nation of Israel (a) the spiritual transformation of a new heart, (b) the forgiveness of their sins, (c) the gathering of the people to the divinely renewed and prosperous land of Canaan, and (d) the establishment of a relationship in which He will be their God and they will be His people.

Although some aspects of these promises have already seen fulfillment,[49] the covenants will be ultimately fulfilled when the Lord establishes the millennial kingdom of Revelation 20:4-6.

III. The Participants of the Millennial Kingdom

In Revelation 20:4, John sees two groups of people reigning with Christ: one group to whom judgment is given and another group made up of the martyrs of the Tribulation (MacLeod 2000: 54-55).[50]

A. The Occupants of the Thrones (20:4a)

1. The occupants of the thrones in verse 4—the ones to whom judgment is given—include the saints of the Old Testament (Dan 7:18), the twelve apostles (Matt 19:28), and the saints of the present age (Rev 2:26-27; 3:21; 5:10; 19:7-8, 14, 19; cf. 1 Cor 6:2) (MacLeod 2000: 55).[51]

2. In other words, the occupants of the thrones—and participants of the kingdom—will include the redeemed of all ages.

B. The Martyrs of the Tribulation (20:4b)

1. The martyrs are those "who had not worshiped the beast or his image, and had not received the mark upon their forehead and upon their hand" (cf. Rev 13:15-18).

2. These believers were beheaded "because of the testimony of Jesus and because of the word of God" (cf. Rev 6:9).

3. After being martyred for their faith and their
   testimony on behalf of Christ, these individuals
   "came to life and reigned with Christ for a
   thousand years."

Their Millennial Functions (Rev 20:4, 6)

According to the Apostle John, these individuals will (a)
occupy thrones and carry out judgment (20:4a),[52] serve as
priests of God and of Christ (20:6b),[53] and reign with
Christ for a thousand years (20:4c, 6c).[54]

Their Blessedness (Rev 20:6)

John declares these individuals to be blessed and holy
because (a) they have been raised from the dead unto
eternal life (20:6a), and (b) they are not subject to the
eternal wrath of God in the lake of fire (20:6b; cf. 2:11).

IV. The Primary Features of the Millennial Kingdom

The two primary features of the millennial kingdom are the
restoration of the nation of Israel and the reign of Jesus
Christ the Messiah.

A. The Restoration of Israel

   1. The Dispersion

      a. Although Yahweh led His people Israel into the
         land of Canaan in faithfulness to His promise
         to Abraham and his descendants, the Jews
         rebelled against God and His law and were
         dispersed from the land in keeping with the
         warnings of Leviticus 26:32-33 and Deutero-
         nomy 28:63-64.[55]

      b. Israel's rebellion and subsequent dispersion,
         however, did not disqualify the nation from the
         covenants of promise. In fact, as Leviticus
         26:40-45 and Deuteronomy 30:1-10 make
         clear, Israel's rebellion and dispersion were
         foreknown by Yahweh and their unfaithfulness
         would *not* cause Him to be unfaithful to His

promises to the nation (see Rom 11:26-29; Ps 89:30-37; Jer 31:35-37).[56]

2. The Restoration

a. In faithfulness to the Abrahamic, Davidic, and New Covenants—as well as to the various promises throughout the prophets of the Old Testament[57]—the Lord will indeed restore the nation of Israel. The only question is when (see Acts 1:6-7).

b. When Israel is restored, she will be brought back to her land; she will be cleansed from her sins; she will be granted a new heart of worship and obedience; and she will enjoy living in peace and prosperity under the rule of the Davidic King (Deut 30:1-10; Jer 23:5-8; Ezek 34:23-24; 36:24-36; 37:24-28).[58]

B. The Reign of Christ

1. When Jesus Christ the Redeemer returns, He will bring about the restoration of Israel in fulfillment of the covenants (Rom 11:26-29) and inaugurate His millennial reign (Rev 19:11-20:6).

2. During the millennial kingdom, Christ will reign in perfect wisdom and will execute justice and righteousness upon the earth. Israel will be saved and dwell securely in the land that He promised them (Jer 33:14-16).

3. This reign of Christ is perhaps most clearly seen in the prophecy of Jeremiah 23:5-8: "'Behold, the days are coming,' declares the Lord, 'when I shall raise up for David a righteous Branch; and He will reign as king and act wisely and do justice and righteousness in the land. In His days Judah will be saved, and Israel will dwell securely; and this is His name by which He will be called, "The Lord our righteousness."' 'Therefore behold, the days are coming,' declares the Lord, 'when they will no longer say, "As the Lord lives, who brought up the sons of Israel from the land of Egypt," but, "As the

Lord lives, who brought up and led back the descendants of the household of Israel from the north land and from all the countries where I had driven them." Then they will live on their own soil.'"

4. The reign of Christ, in other words, will be characterized by an unprecedented justice, peace, and righteousness upon the earth as the glorified Son of God reigns from Jerusalem in perfect wisdom and power, free from Satan's influence in the world.[59]

Conclusion

Scripture indicates that the millennial reign of Christ will take place upon the earth, and that it finds its basis in the Old Testament covenants of promise. In fulfillment of these promises, the divinely redeemed nation of Israel will return to her land where she and all Gentile believers "will experience the personal presence of the living, resurrected Christ in a real, restored Jerusalem. From there Christ will rule and reign with all His saints with an unqualified justice and righteousness such as this old earth has longed to see since the fall of humanity in the Garden of Eden. Great will be the day of our Lord Jesus Christ" (Kaiser 1992: 117).

Chapter 7
The Chronology of Revelation 19-20: Recapitulatory or Sequential?

The Significance of the Question

The question to be considered here concerns the temporal relationship between Revelation 19 and Revelation 20. Do the events recorded in Revelation 20:1-6 follow the events described in Revelation 19:11-21 (the *sequential* view), or does Revelation 20:1 recapitulate and take the reader back to the beginning of the New Testament era (the *recapitulatory* view)?

The Sequential View:

The events of 20:1-6 *follow* those of 19:11-21.

The Recapitulatory View:

The events of 20:1-6 *precede* those of 19:11-21.

The significance of this question is obvious: If the events of Revelation 20:1-6 *follow* Christ's Second Coming in Revelation 19, then the millennium of Revelation 20:1-6 is *not* a present reality and Christ will return *prior* to the millennium (premillennialism).[60]

Millennial View	Recapitulatory	Sequential
Amillennialism	X	
Postmillennialism	X[61]	
Premillennialism		X

The Case for the Sequential Relationship

In examining the temporal relationship between Revelation 19 and Revelation 20, five reasons emerge for affirming a sequential relationship between the two chapters.

I. The Context of Revelation 12-20

The context and flow of Revelation 12-20 point to a chronological relationship in which the events of chapter 20 follow those of chapter 19.

A. In Revelation 12:9, Satan is cast down to the earth where he begins his work of deceiving the whole world.

B. In order to carry out this deception, Satan enlists the beast of the sea (13:1-10) and the beast of the earth (13:11-18), who is later identified as "the false prophet" (16:13; 19:20; 20:10).

C. The three members of this "unholy trinity"—Satan, the beast, and the false prophet—are successful in their attempts to deceive, but they are eventually defeated by Christ, who returns to earth, conquers them, and casts them into the lake of fire in a series of visions in 19:11-20:10.

D. At the conclusion of chapter 19, however, only two-thirds of the "unholy trinity"—the beast and the false prophet—has been defeated and cast into the lake of fire.

What about the fate of Satan?

E. This question is answered beginning in the first verse of Revelation 20.

1. Satan is bound and locked in the abyss to prevent him from deceiving the nations for a thousand years (1-3).

2. After the thousand-year reign (4-6), Satan is released for a short time (7), he resumes his work of deception (8), and he is defeated in his attempt to overthrow the saints (9).

3. Satan is then "thrown into the lake of fire and brimstone, where the beast and the false prophet are also; and they will be tormented day and night forever and ever" (v. 10).

F. Thus, Christ's victory over the beast, the false prophet, and Satan himself is complete.

> So what's the point?

G. The fate of Satan—the remaining one-third of the "unholy trinity"—is *exactly* what the reader would be waiting for and expecting at the beginning of Revelation 20. In other words, "Revelation 20:1-10 serves as the final piece of the puzzle in the defeat and ultimate punishment of the utmost enemy of Christ and His saints. Therefore, in order to make sense of the culminating victory of Christ and conclusive defeat of Satan, Revelation 20:1-10 is a logical and chronological necessity to chapters 12-19" (Hoehner 1992: 247).

H. This, combined with the fact that there is no logical or chronological break at Revelation 20:1 indicated either by the grammar of the text or the surrounding context, demonstrates that the binding of Satan and his subsequent defeat must follow the return of Christ, with which chapter 19 concludes.

II. The Use of "Any Longer" in 20:3

John's use of "any longer" (*eti*) in the purpose clause of Revelation 20:3 strongly suggests that the events described in 20:1-3 follow those described in 19:11-21.

A. This particular use of "any longer" (*eti*) indicates the interruption of something that is already taking place.[62]

B. In other words, when John says that the binding in Revelation 20:3 prevents Satan from deceiving the nations "any longer," the idea is that Satan was engaged in such deception just prior to that binding.

C. This clearly indicates the termination of the deceptive activity referred to in Revelation 19:20 and described in chapters 12-19, and therefore it indicates a sequential relationship of events in chapters 12-20.

   1. Revelation 12:9: Satan is thrown out of heaven, cast down to earth, and described the one "who deceives the whole world."

   2. Revelation 13:14: Satan uses the false prophet, who "deceives those who dwell on the earth."

   3. Revelation 18:23: Satan has used Babylon and her sorcery to deceive "all the nations."

   4. Revelation 19:20: Satan has enabled the false prophet to perform signs "by which he deceived those who had received the mark of the beast and those who worshipped his image."

   5. Revelation 20:3: Satan is bound and imprisoned in the abyss "so that he should not deceive the nations *any longer.*"

D. The use of "any longer" (*eti*) in Revelation 20:3, then, strongly suggests that the binding of Satan in Revelation 20:1-3 follows the events of Revelation 19:11-21.[63]

III. The Description of the Lake of Fire in 20:10

A. When John details the devil's final demise in Revelation 20:10, he writes that Satan "was thrown into the lake of fire and brimstone, where the beast and the false prophet are also."

B. In other words, when Satan is defeated and arrives in the lake of fire, he joins the beast and false prophet who are *already* there (Thomas 1998: 205-06).

C. In this way, the clause "where the beast and the false prophet are also" presupposes an earlier judgment upon the beast and the false prophet (in Rev 19:20) and suggests a sequential relationship between Revelation 19 and 20:

    1. 19:20: The beast and false prophet are thrown into the lake of fire.

    2. 19:21: The enemies of God are destroyed.

    3. 20:1-6: Satan is bound for a thousand years.

    4. 20:7-9: Satan is released and defeated in battle.

    5. 20:10: Satan is cast into the lake of fire, "where the beast and the false prophet are also."

IV. The Absence of Compelling Objections

Despite the many objections, there is simply no compelling reason to abandon the chronologically sequential understanding of the relationship between the events portrayed in chapters 19 and 20.[64]

A. Objection 1:

    1. Articulated: According to the sequential view, Revelation 20:1-3 describes actions taken to prevent Satan's deception of the very nations that had just been destroyed in 19:19-21.

        a. As Poythress notes, "all of Christ's enemies are destroyed in 19:11-21. If 20:1-6 describes events later than 19:11-21, there would be no one left for Satan to deceive in 20:3" (Poythress 2000: 179).

        b. In other words, this objection raises the question: "From where will the nations of Revelation 20:3 and 8 arise?"

2. Considered: The nations of Revelation 20:3 and 8 will arise in one of two ways:

    a. First Possibility: The nations will arise from those who survive the battle in Revelation 19:19-21.[65]

    b. Second Possibility: If Revelation 19 teaches that there are no survivors from the battle, the nations will arise from the offspring of non-glorified believers who originally enter the millennium.[66] According to Thomas, "The only viable alternative is to allow that the battle of 19:19-21 resulted in death for all those not faithful to the Messiah. However, the re-deemed but nonglorified population on earth survives the battle, enters the Millennium (cf. 11:13; 12:13-17), and reproduces offspring some of whom do not become saved as they mature....So a new set of nations will come to exist on earth in a relatively short period" (Thomas 1995: 410-11).[67]

B. Objection 2:

1. Articulated: The parallel between the judgments of Babylon in chapters 17-18, the beast and the false prophet in chapter 19, and Satan in chapter 20 shows that the judgments are arranged themati-cally rather than chronologically.

    According to Poythress, "The judgment of Satan in 20:10 parallels the judgments of Babylon (chap-ters 17-18) and of the Beast and the False Prophet (19:11-21). These enemies of God all receive their doom, and the visions depicting their doom are thematically rather than chronologically arranged" (Poythress 2000: 179).

2. Considered: This argument presupposes what it seeks to prove.

    Poythress provides no evidence that these three judgments are arranged thematically rather than chronologically. Simply stated, there is no compelling reason to deny that these judgments will take place in the order in which they are presented in Revelation 17-20.

C. Objection 3:

1. Articulated: Revelation 20:7-10 is the same battle as the one described in Ezekiel 38-39, which places Revelation 20:7-10 at the end of the present age. Revelation 20:1, then, must recapitulate back to the beginning of the New Testament era.

2. Considered: This objection is answered in one of two ways:

   a. First Possibility: The two battles are not one and the same.[68]

      i. According to Thomas, Revelation 20:7-10 "differs from Ezekiel 38-39 in a number of ways that are sufficient to show this is not specific occasion foreseen by Ezekiel" (Thomas 1995: 424).

      ii. According to this first response, then, because the two passages do not refer to the same battle, this objection poses no problem for the sequential interpretation of Revelation 19-20.

   b. Second Possibility: The two battles are the same, but the battle of Ezekiel 38-39 takes place *after* the millennium.[69]

      i. According to this view, the millennium of Revelation 20:1-6 corresponds to the millennial kingdom described in Ezekiel 36-37, and the battle of Revelation 20:7-10 is the same as that in Ezekiel 38-39.

      ii. The relationship between Revelation 20:1-10 and Ezekiel 36-39, then, would look like this:

Event	Ezek 36-39	Rev 20
Millennium:	ch. 36-37	vv. 1-6
Final Battle:	ch. 38-39	vv. 7-10

iii. This second explanation offers further support for the sequential interpretation of Revelation 19-20, for the final battle of Revelation 20:7-10 is seen to follow the future millennial kingdom of Ezekiel 36-37 and Revelation 20:1-6.

There is, then, no compelling reason to abandon the chronologically sequential understanding of the relationship between the events portrayed in chapters 19 and 20.

V. The Content of the Visions

The content of the visions in Revelation 20:1-6 precludes the possibility that Revelation 20:1 takes the reader back to the beginning of the New Testament era. As discussed in previous chapters:

A. The binding of Satan in Revelation 20:1-3 cannot be reconciled with the New Testament's portrayal of Satan's activities in the present age.

B. The resurrection at the beginning of the thousand years is a bodily one, which establishes that the thousand years do not refer to the current age.

C. The duration of the millennium is one thousand calendar years, which places this time period in the future.

Revelation 20:1, then, does not take the reader back to the beginning of the New Testament era, but rather will be fulfilled *after* the Second Coming of Christ recorded in Revelation 19.

Conclusion

Because the evidence indicates that the events of Revelation 20 follow those described in Revelation (the sequential view), the millennial reign of Christ must take place during a period of time *after* the Second Coming of Christ (the view of premillennialism).

Chapter 8
Satan's Final Battle

The Restriction of Satan (1-6)

The opening six verses of Revelation 20 indicate that Satan
will be prevented from having any kind of influence upon the
earth whatsoever (see chapter 3). During this time, he is
completely restricted.

The Release of Satan (7)

"And when the thousand years are completed, Satan will be
released from his prison..." (7).

I.   In verse 7, what was alluded to at the end of verse 3
     ("after these things he must be released for a short time")
     is now made explicit.

II. Satan does not *escape* from the abyss, but rather is re-
     leased (the verb translated "will be released" is passive)
     by an unnamed agent, presumably the angel of Revelation
     20:1 who holds the key of the abyss. This verse indicates
     God's continual control over Satan, for he is released from
     his imprisonment only when God sees fit.

The Rebellion of Satan (8-9)

"...and will come out to deceive the nations which are in the
four corners of the earth, Gog and Magog, to gather them
together for the war; the number of them is like the sand of

the seashore. And they came up on the broad plain of the earth and surrounded the camp of the saints and the beloved city, and fire came down from heaven and devoured them" (8-9).[70]

I. He Deceives the Nations (8a)

    A. By the end of the millennium, the population of the millennial kingdom will have spread far and wide—to the "four corners of the earth" (v. 8) (Thomas 1995: 423).

        1. Those nations are referred to as "Gog and Magog," names that allude to Ezekiel 38-39 and serve as "emblems for the enemies of Messiah during the end times" (ibid.).[71]

        2. In other words, "Gog and Magog are symbolic figures representing the nations of the world which band together for a final assault upon God and his people. No specific geographical designations are intended. They are simply hostile nations from all across the world" (Mounce 1977: 362).

    B. Those unbelievers in the millennial kingdom who have feigned submission to Christ are easy targets for Satan the deceiver.[72]

    C. After his release from the abyss, "Satan's incurable bent toward evil evidences itself in an immediate return to his efforts to deceive the nations" (Thomas 1995: 423).

II. He Gathers an Army (8b)

Satan is successful in deceiving the nations and is able to gather them together for war against Christ and the saints. The number of his troops is innumerable, "like the sand of the seashore."

III. He Loses the Battle (9)

    A. The Nations Prepare (9a)

1. The saints are gathered together in their "camp"[73] in Jerusalem.

   a. Jerusalem has previously been called the "holy city" (Rev 11:2) and the "great city" (Rev 11:8; 16:19), and now it is called the "beloved city."

   b. According to MacLeod, "It is rightly called 'beloved' because for a thousand years it will have been the seat of Christ's kingdom and the spiritual center of the earth…" (Jer 3:17; 31:6; Micah 4:7; Zech 14:9-11) (MacLeod 2000: 210).

2. The nations surround Christ and the camp of the saints in Jerusalem—a battle is imminent.

B. The Nations Perish (9b)

1. In this, the war to end all wars, the wicked will be destroyed immediately: "fire came down from heaven and devoured them" (v. 9b).

2. This battle is fought not by the saints protecting their city, but by God who sends fire down from heaven—a common form of divine punishment.[74]

3. "The power of God is so great that there will not be even the appearance of a battle" (ibid.).

The Retribution of Satan (10)

"And the devil who deceived them was thrown into the lake of fire and brimstone, where the beast and the false prophet are also; and they will be tormented day and night forever and ever" (10).

I. The Place of the Retribution

   A. Satan will receive his retribution in a place called "the lake of fire and brimstone."

B. This is the place of eternal fire "which has been pre-
pared for the devil" (Matt 25:41) and now opens to
embrace him eternally (Allen 1999: 492).

Consignment to the Lake of Fire	
The Beast	Rev 19:20
The False Prophet	Rev 19:20
Satan	Rev 20:10
Death and Hades	Rev 20:14
Unbelievers	Rev 20:15

II. The Nature of the Retribution

A. Satan—along with the beast and the false prophet—
will be "tormented" during his time in the lake of fire.

1. The word used here means "to torture" or "to
bring about severe distress."

2. Because Satan is a spiritual being, this torment
must be spiritual in nature.[75]

B. This torment is the just punishment for Satan's
wickedness and the ultimate fulfillment of God's
promise in Genesis 3:15 to one day defeat the devil.

III. The Duration of the Retribution

A. The duration of Satan's retribution is captured by the
words "day and night forever and ever" (10).

1. "Day and night" indicates that the torment will be
continual and will not be interrupted by moments
of reprieve.[76]

2. "Forever and ever" indicates that the torment will
last for eternity—it will never end.[77]

B. The retribution of Satan, then, will be continual and
eternal: "There is no intermission and no end" (Morris
1987: 240).

Conclusion

In this vision of the defeat of Satan in the final battle, the Lord demonstrates His sovereignty over the devil and the affairs of this world, giving hope to the present-day believer that God's ultimate victory over evil is assured. In other words, Satan may be alive and *active* on planet earth, but he is not alive and *well*, for his fate has been determined and is quickly drawing near.

Chapter 9
In the Courtroom of God

Introduction

In this final series of visions (vv. 11-15)—which MacArthur refers to as "the most serious, sobering, and tragic passage in the entire Bible" (MacArthur 2000: 245)—John describes the victory of God over the last of His enemies, which ushers in the new heavens and the new earth (Rev 21-22).

The Inescapable Judge (11)

"And I saw a great white throne and Him who sat upon it, from whose presence earth and heaven fled away, and no place was found for them" (11).

I.   The Throne of the Judge (11a)

    A.   The "Throne"

        The throne itself is a symbol of dominion and indicates that its occupant possesses power, rule, and authority, and the right and ability to exercise judgment. This, in other words, is a throne of judgment.

    B.   The "Great" Throne

        The greatness of the throne's size is indicative of the significance of the judgments it will issue forth. As the context will show, this will be the final judgment.

C. The "White" Throne

The throne is white "because of its purity and holiness and righteousness of the verdicts that issue from it" (Thomas 1995: 428). The judgments, in other words, will reflect the character of the Judge Himself.

II. The Identity of the Judge (11b)

A. Throughout the book of Revelation, God the Father is referred to as the One who sits upon the throne (4:2, 3, 9, 10; 5:1, 13; 7:10; 19:4; 21:5).

B. Elsewhere in Scripture, however, it is taught that God the Son is the One who will exercise judgment.

1. John 5:22: The Father "has given all judgment to the Son."

2. John 5:27: The Father "gave Him [Jesus] authority to execute judgment, because He is the Son of Man."

3. Acts 10:42: Peter said: "And He ordered us to preach to the people, and solemnly to testify that this is the One [Jesus] who has been appointed by God as Judge of the living and the dead."

C. Perhaps it is best to say that the Father is "Him who sat upon [the throne]" and that He exercises judgment through the Son, who is also present, but not explicitly mentioned in Revelation 20:11-15.

1. Acts 17:31: God the Father "has fixed a day in which He will judge the world in righteousness *through a Man* whom He has appointed" (emphasis added).

2. Romans 2:16: "God will judge the secrets of men *through Jesus Christ*" (emphasis added).

III. The Description of the Judge (11c)

A. John describes the Judge as the One "from whose presence earth and heaven fled away, and no place was found for them" (11c).

B. This refers to God's judgment of His sin-tainted creation in which heaven and earth are destroyed (cf. 2 Pet 3).

C. The idea, then, is that heaven and earth fled away into nothingness—they dissolved or dissipated—and no place was found for them to exist.[78]

D. As John writes later, "the first heaven and first earth passed away" (Rev 21:1).

The Incontestable Trial (12-13)

"And I saw the dead, the great and the small, standing before the throne, and books were opened; and another book was opened, which is the book of life; and the dead were judged from the things which were written in the books, according to their deeds. And the sea gave up the dead which were in it, and death and Hades gave up the dead which were in them; and they were judged, every one of them according to their deeds" (12-13).

I. The Objects of Judgment (12a, 13a)

A. Their Identity (12a)

1. The objects of judgment are referred to as "the dead." This title refers back to "the rest of the dead" in Revelation 20:5 and has reference to all the unbelievers of all time. In other words, the judgment of Revelation 20:11-15 is the judgment of unbelievers, not believers.[79]

2. The objects of judgment are further described as "the great and the small." This phrase emphasizes that no unbeliever—regardless of his status here on earth—will be exempt from the final judgment. This idea is emphasized further in verse 13b,

where John says that "every one of them" is judged.

B. Their Resurrection (13a)

   1. Scripture teaches that the physical bodies of unbelievers will one day be resurrected.

      a. Daniel 12:2 speaks of a resurrection "to disgrace and everlasting contempt."

      b. John 5:29 speaks of "a resurrection of judgment."

      c. Acts 24:15 speaks of "a resurrection of...the wicked."

   2. This resurrection is described in Revelation 20:13a as "the sea," "Hades," and "death" giving up the dead: "And the sea gave up the dead which were in it, and death and Hades gave up the dead which were in them."

      a. "The sea" literally refers to the sea.

      b. "Hades" most likely refers to the place of the dead (i.e., the grave).[80]

      c. "Death" refers to the condition of being dead.

   3. The idea, then, is that the sea, the grave, and death itself all release the dead bodies that they held captive, and the bodies are raised to stand before the Judge on the great white throne.

II. The Act of Judgment (12b, 13b)

   A. The act of the judgment of the unbelievers is captured in the words "the dead were judged" (12b) and "they were judged" (13b).

   B. The unnamed subject of these passive verbs is God— He is the One who judges.

C. The act of judgment itself consists of God's moral evaluation of unbelievers in accordance with His righteous standard.

III. The Basis of Judgment (12c, 13c)

The basis of God's judgment in John's vision is found in what is written in the *books* (plural) and the *book* (singular).

A. The Books (12c, 13c)

1. At the time of the judgment, God is seen opening the books ("and the books were opened") and He judges the dead "from the things which were written in the books, according to their deeds" (v. 12c).

2. The "books," then, exist as a written record of the deeds they committed during their lives on earth. These include everything the individuals had ever done, said, thought, desired, or purposed in their hearts.

3. Having lived lives of sin, the unbelievers stand guilty before the God of justice and deserving of eternal condemnation.

B. The Book of Life (12c; cf. 15a)

1. The "book of life" is an abbreviation of the title given to this book earlier in Revelation—"the book of life of the Lamb who has been slain" (Rev 13:8).

2. This book is a divine register that contains the name of every individual who has received eternal life through faith in Jesus Christ, the Lamb of God who was slain on behalf of sinners.

The *books* (plural) and the *book* (singular), then, serve as a dual witness against the unbelievers: Not only have they committed innumerable acts of wickedness before the Lord, but they have also refused to take refuge in the Lamb of God who takes away the sin of the world.

**The Chronology of the Events
in Revelation 20:11-13**

1. The unbelievers are resurrected (13a).
2. The unbelievers stand before God's throne.
3. Heaven and earth are judged (11b).
4. John sees unbelievers before God's throne (12a).
5. The unbelievers are judged (12b, 13b).

The Irreversible Sentence (14-15)

"And death and Hades were thrown into the lake of fire. This is the second death, the lake of fire. And if anyone's name was not found written in the book of life, he was thrown into the lake of fire" (14-15).

I.   The Objects of the Sentence (14a, 15a)

    A.   Death and Hades (14a)

        1.   The casting of death and Hades into the lake of fire indicates the destruction of death itself.

        2.   In other words, no longer will death and the grave ("Hades") have power to take lives.

        3.   This later serves as a comforting assurance to those who inherit the new heaven and the new earth in the eternal state: "He shall wipe away every tear from their eyes; and *there shall no longer be any death*; there shall no longer be any mourning, or crying, or pain; the first things have passed away" (Rev 21:4; emphasis added).

        4.   In other words, this marks the Lord's victory over death itself.

    B.   Unbelievers (15a)

        1.   Unbelievers are here described as those whose names are not found written in the book of life.

2. As stated previously, these are those individuals who have refused to take refuge in the Lamb of God who takes away the sin of the world.

II. The Place of the Sentence (14b, 15b)

   A. The place of the sentence is said to be "the lake of fire."

      1. This graphic title for hell is reminiscent of descriptions elsewhere in the New Testament:

         a. "the fire" (Matt 3:10; 7:19)

         b. "unquenchable fire" (Matt 3:12)

         c. "the fiery hell" (Matt 5:22; 18:9; cf. James 3:6)

         d. "the furnace of fire" (Matt 13:42, 50)

         e. "the eternal fire" (Matt 18:8; 25:41)

         f. "the unquenchable fire" (Mark 9:43; cf. Mark 9:48)

         g. "the punishment of eternal fire" (Jude 7)

         h. "the fury of a fire which will consume the adversaries" (Heb 10:27)

         i. "the lake of fire which burns with brimstone" (Rev 19:20)

         j. "the lake of fire and brimstone" (Rev 20:10)

         k. "the lake that burns with fire and brimstone" (Rev 21:8)

      2. Other descriptions of hell in the New Testament do not contain references to fire but are equally as graphic:

    a. "the outer darkness" where there will be "weeping and gnashing of teeth" (Matt 22:13; 25:30; cf. Matt 13:42)

    b. "eternal punishment" (Matt 25:46)

    c. "eternal destruction, away from the presence of the Lord and from the glory of His power" (2 Thess 1:9)

    d. "eternal judgment" (Heb 6:2)

    e. "the black darkness" (2 Pet 2:17; Jude 13)

B. There has been some discussion regarding whether the fire is literal or symbolic.

    1. If taken literally, the lake of fire includes actual fire that will inflict punishment upon the wicked.

    2. If taken symbolically, the "lake of fire" communicates that hell will be a place of unspeakable torment, but not a place of actual fire.

C. At the outset, it is noted that the phrase "the lake of fire" should at least be considered a "candidate" for symbolic language, for it does possess some degree of absurdity when taken literally and some degree of clarity when taken symbolically.

    1. The absurdity of the literal interpretation has been noted in three ways.

        a. How can hell include literal fire when it is also described as a place of darkness? The two are mutually exclusive concepts (Crockett 1992: 59-60).

        b. How can hell include punishment by literal fire when Matthew 25:41 says that the eternal fire was created for spirit beings like the devil and his angels (cf. Rev 20:10)? Physical fire works on physical bodies with physical nerve endings, and Satan and his demons do not possess these (Crockett 1992: 30).

   c. How can hell include literal fire and be eternal? Wouldn't the bodies of the wicked burn up and exist no more after a period of time?[81]

2. The clarity of the symbolic interpretation is indisputable: it indicates that hell is a place of unspeakable torment where its occupants will undergo extreme pain and suffering.

D. In addition, the very idea of a "lake" of fire suggests that the language may be symbolic (i.e., lakes usually contain water, not fire).[82]

E. At the same time, other factors support the interprettation that the fire is indeed literal.

1. The number of references to fire in connection with eternal punishment (Matt 3:10, 12; 5:22; 7:19; 13:42, 50; 18:8, 9; 25:41; Mark 9:43, 48; Heb 10:27; James 3:6; Rev 19:20; 21:8) suggests that literal fire is indeed intended (Walvoord 1992: 28).

2. The fact that the unbelievers are resurrected bodily prior to being judged and cast into the lake of fire indicates that their punishment there will be physical as well as spiritual.

   a. As Wallace notes, "one has to answer the question: Why, then, are non-believers resurrected if hell is only spiritual? The whole point of the resurrection is to reunite body and soul. God could easily send souls directly to hell. But he does not. He raises all people from the dead and then sends that person to hell" (Wallace 2001: 3).[83]

   b. Because punishment in hell will be physical as well as spiritual, it would make sense that the fire mentioned throughout the New Testament is literal fire.

F. Regardless of whether or not the fire is literal, the point is clear—the pain and agony of those tormented in the lake of fire will be unspeakable.

III. The Duration of the Sentence (14b, 15b; cf. 14:11; 20:10)

A. Although the duration of the sentence is not explicitly stated in Revelation 20:14-15, other descriptions of the lake of fire in Revelation make it clear that the sentence is an eternal one—it will last forever.

1. Revelation 14:11: "And the smoke of their torment goes up *forever and ever*; and they have no rest day and night, those who worship the beast and his image, and whoever receives the mark of his name" (emphasis added).

2. Revelation 20:10: "And the devil who deceived them was thrown into the lake of fire and brimstone, where the beast and the false prophet are also; and they will be tormented day and night *forever and ever*" (emphasis added).

B. The eternal duration of the punishment of the wicked can be seen in other New Testament descriptions of hell.

1. "unquenchable fire" (Matt 3:12; Mark 9:43)

2. "the eternal fire" (Matt 18:8; 25:41)

3. "the punishment of eternal fire" (Jude 7)

4. "eternal punishment" (Matt 25:46)

5. "eternal destruction" (2 Thess 1:9)

6. "eternal judgment" (Heb 6:2)

C. The reference to "eternal punishment" in Matthew 25:46 in particular makes it clear that the duration of the punishment is eternal.

1. In this verse, Jesus says, "And these [unbelievers] will go away into eternal punishment, but the righteous into eternal life."

2. The parallel structure of Jesus' statement makes it clear that the duration of "eternal punishment" is the same as that of "eternal life."

The punishment that the wicked experience in the lake of fire, then, will go on forever and ever.[84]

Conclusion

As Revelation 20 comes to a close, then, the Lord is seen to be victorious over everything that is tainted by sin and wickedness—the beast and the false prophet, Satan, heaven and earth, unbelievers, and even death itself. Only those whose robes have been washed white in the blood of the Lamb (Rev 7:14; 22:14) shall inherit the blessings of the new heaven and the new earth in the eternal state:

Revelation 21:1-4

(1) And I saw a new heaven and a new earth; for the first heaven and the first earth passed away, and there is no longer any sea. (2) And I saw the holy city, new Jerusalem, coming down out of heaven from God, made ready as a bride adorned for her husband. (3) And I heard a loud voice from the throne, saying, "Behold, the tabernacle of God is among men, and He shall dwell among them, and they shall be His people, and God Himself shall be among them, (4) and He shall wipe away every tear from their eyes; and there shall no longer be any death; there shall no longer be any mourning, or crying, or pain; the first things have passed away."

In the words of the Apostle John: "Come, Lord Jesus" (Rev 22:20).

Endnotes

Chapter 1: Introduction to Eschatology

[1] Although this chart indicates that the resurrection of believers takes place at the Second Coming of Christ, premillennialists who hold to a pre-tribulational rapture believe that the church will be resurrected *prior* to the seven years of tribulation and not after it. This chart is intentionally simplistic because it is designed to present premillennialism in a way that clearly distinguishes it from postmillennialism and amillennialism, not in a way that sets forth any of the rapture views.

Chapter 2: Introduction to Revelation

[2] For evidence for the later date, see Thomas 1992: 20-23, Carson, Moo, and Morris 1992: 473-76, and Hiebert 1977: 253-57.

Chapter 3: The Timing of Satan's Binding

[3] Some postmillennialists understand Satan to have been bound at the time of Christ's victory on the cross, while others see the binding of Satan to represent a future point in time when the successful proclamation of the gospel will have effectively reduced Satan's influence to nothing (Gregg 1997: 457). Because postmillennialists teach that the present age

gradually merges into the millennium, the precise time of the binding is not always emphasized in their writings.

[4] Strimple explains the binding of Satan in a similar fashion: "The age of salvation for the Gentiles has arrived. Prior to Christ's ministry Israel was the one nation called out from all the nations of the world to know God's blessings and to serve him. There were exceptions, of course—those who came to know God's grace even though they were not of the children of Abraham after the flesh. But essentially all the nations on this earth were in darkness, under Satan's deception. But then, praise God! Christ came and accomplished his redemptive work....The age of world missions had begun, and Satan's deceptive work on that grand scale over so many centuries had come to an end" (Strimple 1999: 123-24). This understanding of the binding of Satan in Revelation 20 is also articulated by Garlington (1997: 72), Gentry (1998: 83 and 1999: 52-53), Hamilton (1955: 131), and Hoekema (1979: 228-29).

[5] According to Beasley-Murray, "A seal on a prison door ensured that prisoners could not escape unobserved. Only he who authorized the imprisonment could authorize release from it (see Dan. 6:17; Mt. 27:66)" (Beasley-Murray 1974: 285).

[6] The word "abyss" (*abussos*) was originally an adjective "meaning *bottomless, unfathomable*, then a noun signifying *a deep place*" (Liefeld 1976: 30). It refers to a prison for spirits in Luke 8:31; Revelation 9:1-2, 11; 11:7; 17:8; and 20:1 and 3, and it refers to the realm of the dead in Romans 10:7. That its use in Revelation 20:1 and 3 refers to a spirit prison is clear from Revelation 20:7, where it is called Satan's "prison."

[7] In arguing that Satan's present-day activities are not in conflict with his present-day imprisonment in Revelation 20, Hendriksen writes, "A dog...bound with a long and heavy chain can do great damage within the circle of his imprisonment" (Hendriksen 1967: 190). What Hendriksen seems to ignore, however, is that Satan's "circle of imprisonment" is identified in verse 3 as the *abyss*. If Satan is free to roam and do damage *only* in the abyss, then he is indeed cut off from activity on the earth. In similar fashion, Cox writes, "Satan, though bound, still goes about like a roaring lion seeking whom he may devour. The chain with which he is bound is a long one, allowing him much freedom of movement" (Cox

1966: 139). Rather than regarding the chain as the means by which Satan is bound (tied up), Cox writes as if the imagery were one of Satan on a leash. The "length" of the chain is not only unstated, it is irrelevant, for the imagery is one of Satan being *bound* by it and then locked and sealed in an escape-proof prison. What indication is there, in the language of Revelation 20:1-3, that Satan has "much freedom of movement"? Simply stated, there is none.

[8] Another objection comes from Jude 6, which states, "And angels who did not keep their own domain, but abandoned their proper abode, He has kept in eternal bonds under darkness for the judgment of the great day." Regarding Jude 6 and its implications for a correct understanding of Revelation 20:1-3, Grenz writes, "Just as the demons in chains are not totally powerless, but restricted in activity, so also the binding of Satan entails restriction rather than total incapacitation" (Grenz 1992: 162; see Strimple 1999: 124, for a fuller discussion of this point).

In response, it must first be stated that there are two main views regarding the identity of the angels in Jude 6 (Hiebert 1989: 234). According to the first view, Jude 6 is a reference to the original fall of the angels who defected with Satan. According to the second view, the angels are the "sons of God" in Genesis 6:2 who "took wives for themselves" from the daughters of men and were thus imprisoned by God as described in Jude 6. While settling the interpretive issue in Jude 6 is beyond the scope of this study, two simple points can be made: (1) If the angels in Jude 6 are the "sons of God" in Genesis 6:2, then Grenz's argument loses all force, for Jude 6 would be saying that only *some*, and not all, of the angels/demons are in "eternal bonds." (2) If Jude 6 refers to the original fall of Satan and his angels, then it cannot refer to confinement in the *abyss*. This is true for two reasons: (a) If Jude 6 refers to the original fall, then Satan himself was also placed into eternal bonds with the rest of his angels. In this case, Jude 6 couldn't be a reference to the *abyss*, for Satan is not thrown into the abyss until the vision of Revelation 20:1-3 takes place. (b) Luke 8:31 and Revelation 9 make it clear that not all demons are in the abyss. Thus, Grenz's argument fails to prove that Satan's binding in Revelation 20:1-3 involves "restriction rather than total incapacitation."

[9] In this passage, Paul describes how unbelievers of the present age respond to Christ and the message of His gospel.

The verb translated "has blinded" is the aorist indicative of *tuphloo*, which literally means "to blind or deprive of sight" (Bauer, Arndt, and Gingrich 1979: 831). Here *tuphloo* is used metaphorically and carries the meaning, "to cause someone not to be able to understand" (Louw and Nida 1989: 1:386). The idea in 2 Corinthians 4:4, then, is that Satan actively exerts a deceptive influence over the minds of unbelievers that prevents them from apprehending the truth and glory of the gospel. According to this verse Satan is clearly at work deceiving unbelievers in the present age.

In arguing for a present-day imprisonment of Satan, Cox explains that Revelation 20:3 means that Satan "can no longer deceive the nations by keeping the gospel from them" (Cox 1966: 62; cf. Boettner 1977: 203). Deception, however, has nothing to do with preventing words of truth from being spoken to unbelievers and everything to do with preventing them from believing the truth when they do hear it. Perhaps it might be argued that while Satan is unable to deceive *the nations* during the present age, he *is* able to deceive *individual believers*. Townsend's response is fitting: "The New Testament makes it clear that Satan is now very much involved in the deception of the nations, for what is the deception of the nations if it is not the deception of individuals who make up the nations?" (Townsend 1983: 217)

[10] The noun translated "snare" in this verse is *pagis*, which literally refers to a snare or trap that was used to catch birds (Hartley and Hickcox 1988: 556; Louw and Nida 1989: 1:56). In this context it is used figuratively of "the intellectual allurement of error" and refers to a trap that Satan sets for unbelievers (Knight 1992: 425). In this verse, Paul expresses his desire that a gentle correction of unbelievers who oppose the truth might break them out of the intoxicating effect of Satan's snare and bring them to their senses and a knowledge of the truth (ibid.). It is clear that the unbelievers described in this verse are objects of Satan's deceptive work as he holds them captive to error.

[11] If Satan is presently bound and unable to deceive according to Revelation 20:1-3, what is the basis of Paul's concern for the Corinthians in this verse? The fear of the apostle expressed in this verse demonstrates that Satan continues to deceive as he did back in Eden and that he is therefore not bound and imprisoned in the abyss at the present time.

Although it may be argued that Paul's concern is that false teachers (not Satan) might deceive his beloved Corinthians, verse 15 of the same chapter makes it clear that these false teachers are the instruments of Satan himself.

[12] Venema also asserts that the restriction is merely a matter of degree, writing, "Satan is bound so that he can neither prevent the spread of the gospel among the nations nor *effectively* deceive them" (Venema 2000: 319; emphasis added). Venema here implies that Satan is still able to deceive the nations, but not as effectively as he did in the past.

[13] Some have argued that Revelation 20:3 does not refer to deception *per se*, but rather to "deceiving the nations in such a way as to gather them together for an all-out assault against God's saints..." (Strimple 1999: 273; cf. Morris 1987: 229; Garlington 1997: 72; Hoekema 1979: 228). According to this view, the deception in Revelation 20:3 is different from the kind of general deception referred to in passages such as 2 Corinthians 4:3-4, 2 Timothy 2:26, 2 Corinthians 11:3, Revelation 12:9, 13:14, and 16:13-16. These New Testament passages are said to be irrelevant to the correct understanding of Revelation 20:3, because they do not refer to a deception in which those deceived are led into an all-out assault against the church. Evidence that the deception of Revelation 20:3 is limited in this way has been supplied from Revelation 20:7-8, which says that once that Satan *is* released, he will begin to deceive the nations in this very way (i.e., he will lead the nations into battle against the saints).

The problem with this view is found in the words "any longer" in Revelation 20:3, which says that the purpose of Satan's binding and imprisonment is "that he should not deceive the nations *any longer.*" When it is used temporally with a negative particle (as it is here: *me...eti*), *eti* (translated "any longer") denotes the interruption of something that is already taking place (Ostella 1975: 236-38; cf. Bauer, Arndt, and Gingrich 1979: 315; Abbott-Smith 1986: 183). Therefore, those amillennialists who believe that the deception in Revelation 20:3 refers specifically and exclusively to a deception that leads the nations into an all-out assault against the church must be willing to assert that the nations were already in the process of being deceived and led into this kind of battle at the time that Satan was incarcerated during Christ's first-century ministry. Simply stated, this assertion cannot be supported by Scripture, and this argument, therefore, loses its force.

[14] As Barbieri writes, "by driving out demons, He was proving He was greater than Satan. He was able to go into Satan's realm (the strong man's house), the demonic world, and come away with the spoils of the victory (12:29). Since He could do this, He was able to institute the kingdom of God among them (v. 28). If He were driving out demons by Satan's power, He certainly could not be offering the people God's kingdom. That would be contradictory. The fact that He was coming to establish the kingdom clearly showed that He worked by the power of the Spirit of God, not by Satan's power" (Barbieri 1983: 46).

[15] According to Boer, "The binding of the strong man in the Synoptic Gospels...bears no recognizable relationship to the thrust of the amillennial view. That thrust is that the binding of Satan applies...to his ability to deceive the nations. But where are the nations in the pericopes that refer to the binding of the strong man? They are not to be seen. What is very much in view is the local sufferers from demon possession and Satan's inability to prevent Jesus from healing them; what is not at all in view is the now blessedly undeceived nations" (Boer 1975: 29). In other words, that Satan is bound in Matthew 12 means that Jesus had the power to plunder the strong man's house (i.e., deliver those under his control) any time He wanted. In Revelation 20, however, the effects of the binding consist of the absolute inability of Satan to deceive the nations during the thousand-year period. The inability of Satan to stop Jesus from delivering demoniacs is not the same as his inability to deceive the nations.

[16] The binding of Satan in Matthew 12:29 did not actually eliminate Satan's ability to control individuals through demon possession. If it had, the exorcisms would have been unnecessary, for every demon possessing an individual would have had to abandon its victim the moment the strong man was bound. The binding referred to in Matthew 12:29, then, does not mean Satan is unable to wield influence on the earth (as it does in Rev 20:1-3). Instead, it means that Jesus possessed the ability to deliver those under Satan's control, and that Satan was unable to stop Him.

[17] This conclusion reflects a different hermeneutical approach than the one taken by most amillennialists. Rather than using Matthew 12:29 to interpret Revelation 20:1-3—as most amillennialists do—this approach seeks to interpret both

passages in their own individual contexts and then compare them to see if they are indeed parallel to one another.

[18] The difficulty in responding to the argument from Luke 10:17-18 stems from the failure of those who advance this argument to explain exactly *how* Jesus' statement makes their case. For example, although Hendriksen refers to Luke 10:17-18 as "a very significant passage which will do much to explain Rev. 20," (Hendriksen 1967: 225), he never does explain precisely how the two relate or what contribution Luke 10:17-18 makes to the correct interpretation of Revelation 20:1-3. If the argument is that the "falling" of Satan in Luke 10:18 is the same as the "throwing" of Satan into the abyss in Revelation 20:3, this must be specifically proven from the texts themselves and not simply assumed.

Chapter 4: The Nature of the First Resurrection

[19] Although most postmillennialists affirm either view 1 or view 2 as described later in this chapter (both of which interpret the first resurrection as spiritual), others do not fit neatly into one of these two categories. For example, some postmillennialists believe that the first resurrection refers to a rebirth of the cause for which the martyrs died, others believe it refers to a revival of the martyr spirit within the church, and still others believe it may refer back to Christ's own resurrection (in which every believer has a part) (Gregg 1997: 465, 67). All postmillennialists are united, however, in their rejection of the physical resurrection view.

[20] As Hamilton asks regarding 1 John 3:14, "What else can we call passing 'out of death into life,' but resurrection?" (Hamilton 1955: 120).

[21] At the same time, it is possible that John is using the word "resurrection" in a unique way in Revelation 20, for the term *would* be a fitting way to refer to the new birth. This argument against view 1, then, is not conclusive. However, it does place the burden of proof on those who insist on this interpretation of the word.

[22] In referring to the thousand years, John uses an accusative of time, which indicates an *extent* of time (Wallace 1996: 202-03). Therefore, as Powell notes, "Satan is imprison-

ed for the extent of the entire 1000-year period, and for this same time period the saints reign with Christ" (Powell 2001: 10). Had John intended to indicate that the saints reigned *during* the thousand years (as views 1 and 2 teach) instead of throughout the entirety of the thousand years, the *genitive* of time would have been more suitable (ibid.). Incidentally, according to Powell, "All other occurrences of groups or plural subjects with the accusative of extent of time in the NT have the entire group beginning and ending the period of time together" (ibid.; cf. Matt 20:6; 28:20; John 2:12; 11:6; Acts 21:7; Rev 2:10 and 9:10).

[23] This interpretation of *zao* in 1 Peter 4:6 is based upon the understanding that the phrase "in the spirit" refers to being in the spiritual *realm* (i.e., in *heaven*) as opposed to being "in the flesh" (in 4:1 and 4:6) (i.e., on earth in this present life). The use of *zao* in Luke 20:38 needs no explanation.

[24] The key word in verse 5 is "until" ("*until* after the thousand years were completed"). Hoekema and other proponents of view 2 believe that the use of the word "until" (*achri*) "does not imply that these unbelieving dead will reign and live with Christ after this period has ended" (Hoekema 1979: 236). In other words, the word *achri* means "up to a certain point" and does not itself determine the state of affairs after the time period has ended (i.e., it does not contemplate a change after the thousand years are completed). Therefore, it simply means that dead unbelievers will share nothing of the new kind of heavenly life that is enjoyed by believers in the present age (i.e., for them, there is no second resurrection).

Although the word "until" (*achri*) can be used in this way, this understanding of the word is difficult to sustain in this context for six reasons: (1) When "until" (*achri*) is used as a conjunction (as it is here in Rev 20:5) rather than as an improper preposition, it refers to a period of time that will come to an end and be followed by a change of those circumstances (Deere 1978: 68-69; cf. Bauer, Arndt, and Gingrich 1979: 128-29; Blaising 1999: 225-26; and MacLeod 2000: 58). This confronts Hoekema with an insurmountable theological problem, for his interpretation implies "the unbelieving dead of verse 5 live spiritually in heaven like the martyrs of verse 4 after the thousand years is completed" (Deere 1978: 68). This amounts to universalism. (2) The exact same expressions are used in 20:3 and 20:5 ("until the thousand years were completed") and 20:3 clearly contemplates a change after the thousand years are completed. This strongly implies that the rest of dead will indeed *ezesan* ("come to life" or "live") after the thousand-year period. (3) "If John simply wanted to deny the resurrection and reign to the others, he could easily have said, 'The rest of the dead did not come to life.' The addition of 'until the thousand years were ended' clearly suggests subsequent action" (Saucy 1993: 276), whereas the clause is superfluous if subsequent action is not intended. (4) If neither use of *ezesan* refers to a bodily resurrection, then there is no mention of the future resurrect-tion of the believer in Revelation 20. This is possible, but perhaps not probable. (5) This interpretation raises the ques-tion of why John would have deemed it necessary to inform or assure his readers that unbelievers will not enter heaven and enjoy life there with Christ. There is no reason to believe that such a possibility would have entered their minds. (6) A *first* resurrection simply implies a second one. As Saucy states, "the immediate identification of the coming to life of the first group as the 'first' resurrection seems clearly to suggest a second resurrection involving those remaining" (ibid.). There-fore, the claim that verse 5 makes no reference to a second resurrection is erroneous and cannot be supported by the text itself.

[25] See endnote 22 above.

[26] An additional difficulty for views 1 and 2 is the New Testament teaching that the believer's reign with Christ is future, not present (2 Tim 2:12). For evidence that believers are not presently reigning with Christ, see Saucy 1993: 105-06.

[27] For evidence that the believers who reign on earth are not limited to those believers martyred during the Great Tribulation, but rather will include the redeemed of all ages, see chapter six.

[28] Grudem's insights on John 5 are helpful: "The fact that Jesus says in this context, 'The *hour* is coming when all who are in the tombs will hear his voice' does not require that both resurrections happen at the same time, for the word *hour* elsewhere in John's gospel can refer to a long period of time; just three verses previously, Jesus said, 'Truly, truly, I say to you, the *hour* is coming, and now is, when the dead will hear

the voice of the Son of God, and those who hear will live' (John 5:25). Here the 'hour' refers to the entire church age when those who are spiritually dead hear Jesus' voice and come to life. John can also use the word *hour*...to speak of the time when true worshipers worship the Father in spirit and in truth (John 4:21, 23), or when intense persecution will come on the disciples (John 16:2). These examples also speak of long periods of time, even entire ages" (Grudem 1994: 1119). In similar fashion, Blaising cites 1 John 2:18 ("it is the last hour") and writes, "If the eschatological hour can be extended over two thousand years, it is not impossible that a thousand years might transpire between the resurrection of the just and the resurrection of the unjust" (Blaising 1999: 150).

[29] As Grudem writes, "All of these verses, in the absence of Revelation 20:5-6, might or might not be speaking of a single future time of resurrection. But with the explicit teaching of Revelation 20:5-6 about two resurrections, these verses must be understood to refer to the future certainty of a resurrection for each type of person, without specifying that those resurrections will be separated in time" (Grudem 1994: 1120).

Similar to this is the portrayal of the coming of Messiah in the Old Testament, which contains no clear evidence "that this would be accomplished in separate events as indicated in the New Testament (cf. Isa 61:1-4; Zech 9:9-10)" (Saucy 1993: 89). As Saucy notes, "It is only with the New Testament that we learn that this involves two stages separated around two appearances of the Messiah" (ibid.). Amillennialist Anthony Hoekema expresses the same basic perspective concerning the coming of the Messiah, writing, "In the New Testament we...find the realization that what the Old Testament writers seemed to depict as one movement must now be recognized as involving two stages: the present Messianic age and the age of the future" (Hoekema 1979: 89). A similar phenomenon exists with the resurrection of the just and the unjust: In the New Testament (and specifically Rev 20) one finds that what the Old Testament writers seemed to depict as one movement must now be recognized as involving two stages: the resurrection of the just and then the resurrection of the unjust a thousand years later. Hoekema and other non-premillennialists recognize this phenomenon with the coming of Messiah but not with the future resurrections of the righteous and the wicked. For a helpful discussion of this phenomenon in Scripture, see Wallace 2002.

[30] In the Greek language, only the imperfect and aorist tenses are used to express the ingressive idea. As Wallace notes, "The difference between the ingressive *imperfect* and the ingressive *aorist* is that the imperfect stresses the beginning, but implies that the action *continues*, while the aorist stresses beginning, but does not imply that the action continues" (Wallace 1996: 544). Because the resurrection at the beginning of the thousand years is not a *continuous* resurrection (i.e., those individuals will not *continue* to come to life over an extended period of time), the aorist tense is the most obvious choice to express the ingressive idea. It should also be noted that the ingressive aorist is also commonly used with *stative* verbs (ibid., 558), such as *zao*.

Chapter 5: The Duration of the Thousand Years

[31] The premillennial interpretation is not dependent on the literal understanding of the thousand years, which can be seen in the fact that not all premillennialists insist on interpreting the thousand years literally (e.g, Ladd 1972: 262; Grudem 1994: 1131; Bock 1999: 304; Blaising 1999: 227).

[32] Because postmillennialists believe that the exact starting point of the millennium is difficult (if not impossible) to discern, postmillennialism does not necessarily require that the thousand years be taken symbolically. The symbolic view, however, is the interpretation generally held by its proponents.

[33] For amillennialists and some postmillennialists, it consists of the *entire* period between the first and second comings, but for other postmillennialists it refers to a period of time that begins *some time after* the first coming and extends to the Second Coming (see endnote 32 above).

[34] Some seem to believe that if *anything* in a given passage is symbolic, then *everything* must be symbolic (e.g., Poythress 1993: 41-54). In contrast, the approach recommended here can be illustrated by considering the statement, "It was raining cats and dogs outside." Interpreter #1 looks at the statement and says, "Well, if it says that it was raining cats and dogs, then actual cats and dogs must have been falling from the sky!" Interpreter #2 looks at it and says, "Well, since it's obviously not raining literal cats and literal

dogs, then it must not be raining at all. Therefore, we must address the question of what the rain symbolizes." Both interpreters are in error because both take an "all-or-nothing" approach to interpreting the statement in question. The key to a correct interpretation is (a) to recognize that there can be both literal and figurative elements in the same text and (b) to seek to discern which aspects of the text fall into which category. In this illustration, for example, "It was raining...outside" should be taken *literally*, and the "cats and dogs" should be taken *figuratively*. Both the literal and the figurative function together to communicate that it was raining very hard.

[35] This, in itself, does not prove that the "thousand years" should be taken literally, but it is a good place to start when seeking to discern the meaning of the designation.

After listing and discussing Deuteronomy 7:9, Exodus 20:5-6, Psalm 50:10-11, Psalm 84:10, Psalm 90:4, and 2 Peter 3:8, Venema states that these passages indicate "that the number one thousand is often used in the Scriptures to refer to an extensive period of time" (Venema 2000: 326). Only three of these passages (Psalm 84:10, Psalm 90:4, and 2 Peter 3:8), however, refer to periods of time, and in all three the number one thousand is intended literally (see endnote 36 below for a brief discussion of these verses).

Of the three remaining passages—Deuteronomy 7:9, Exodus 20:5-6, and Psalm 50:10—Exodus 20:5-6 can be quickly dismissed, for in it the indefinite figure "thousands" is used rather than the specific number *one thousand*. In Deuteronomy 7:9 and Psalm 50:10, however, the number seems to be used to indicate an indefinite amount (cf. Davis 1941: 54), although the figure could be understood literally in Psalm 50:10. These two verses, then, give the strongest support to the possibility that the designation "a thousand years" in Revelation 20 is not intended literally, and a possibility it is. The reason the symbolic view is rejected here is that it is not warranted by the context in the way that it is in Deuteronomy 7:9 and (possibly) in Psalm 50:10 (see letter F on pages 48-50).

[36] The idea of 2 Peter 3:8, which is an amplification of Psalm 90:4 (Hiebert 1989: 153), is that the delay of a (literal) thousand years may well seem like a (literal) day against the backdrop of eternity (Green 1987: 146). Perhaps what confuses the one who takes the "thousand years" in 2 Peter 3:8 symbolically is the fact that it seems that Peter could have just

as easily selected the phrase "a *hundred* years" and still made his point. While this is true, it does not discount the fact that Peter is using the number literally in this verse. To illustrate, if Jim makes the statement, "I wish I had a million dollars," his friend Steve might think that he's not referring to a *literal* million dollars. "After all," Steve might reason, "Jim merely means to say that he wishes he was very rich." While it may be true that Jim is expressing his desire to be wealthy, it is also true that he is doing so by expressing his desire for a *literal* million dollars!

In similar fashion, the psalmist's point in Psalm 84:10 is that one (literal) day in God's courts is better than a (literal) thousand days in any other place. There is nothing in any of these three texts that compels the interpreter to seek a meaning other than the literal one.

[37] It should be noted that this method of argumentation—"if John had meant such-and-such, he would have certainly written it in such-and-such a way"—is usually less than conclusive, and that is the case here as well.

[38] It should be noted that the possession of these two characteristics does not *necessitate* that a given text be taken figuratively, for many supernatural truths may seem absurd to the mind of man. At the same time, however, the *absence* of these two characteristics would seem to indicate that the language in question is not symbolic in nature. In this way, one might say that a given statement must possess these two characteristics in order to be considered a *candidate* for symbolic language.

[39] This verse highlights well the inadequacy of the strictly "literal-if-possible" approach to interpreting Scripture. If that approach were taken with Isaiah 55:12, the interpreter might take the statement about trees clapping their hands literally. After all, nothing is impossible with God, and so it is *possible* that the trees could grow hands and begin clapping them!

[40] To use an illustration from the text in question, the "great chain" in Revelation 20:1-2 possesses both a degree of absurdity when taken literally (i.e., "How could a *physical* chain be used to bind a *spiritual* being?") and a degree of clarity when taken symbolically (i.e., it clearly communicates that Satan is immobilized).

[41] Perhaps an amillennialist's *eschatology* might cause him to scratch his head and wonder, "How can this be?," but exegesis must determine one's theology, and not vice versa.

[42] Amillennialist Stanley Grenz's argument *in favor of* the symbolic interpretation of the "thousand years" actually illustrates this point well. He writes: "Like the book as a whole, chapter 20 is highly symbolic. It speaks of Satan being bound with a chain and cast into a bottomless pit, and it anticipates a second death that lasts forever. The author obviously intended that none of these be interpreted in a purely literal manner, as such an interpretation would be nonsensical–that is, a spiritual being bound with a physical chain and confined in a physical pit with no bottom. Consequently, it is possible that other figures in these verses, including the thousand years, are likewise to be understood symbolically" (Grenz 1992: 167). Notice that Grenz concludes that the chain must be interpreted *symbolically* because the literal interpretation is "nonsensical." With this as his litmus test, one wonders why he concludes that the "thousand years" is to be interpreted symbolically, for there is nothing nonsensical about taking it literally.

[43] Hoekema and Warfield trace the number one thousand back to the cube of ten, which is the sum of seven plus three (Hoekema 1979: 227; Warfield 1929: 654). As Erickson notes, however, "One might question why, in attempting to discern the meaning of the number ten, we should investigate the meaning of seven and three instead of, say, six and four..." (Erickson 1998: 84). Or one might even question why the number one thousand would drive someone to discern the meaning of the number ten! Furthermore, what is the significance of the number ten being *cubed?* As Deere asks, "Why not ten to the fourth or fifth degree, or better still, ten to the tenth degree?" (Deere 1978: 70) Such questions are not meant to badger or mock those who interpret the thousand years symbolically, but only to illustrate the chaos and confusion that is introduced when one attempts to explain the significance of the "thousand years" as a symbol. This, in itself, weighs heavily against rejecting the literal interpretation of the time period.

Several proponents of the symbolic interpretation assert that the number one thousand denotes *completeness* and thus the "thousand years" refers to *a complete period of time* (Hoekema 1979: 227; Cox 1966: 4; Boettner 1957: 64). In response, however, one wonders what exactly *is* "a complete period of time." What would constitute an *incomplete* period of time, and how would it differ from a *complete* period of time? What exactly is being communicated in the six-fold use of the "thousand years"? One commentator refers to the "thousand years" as "the complete time that God has determined" (Morris, *Revelation*, 229), but what meaning does this actually communicate? What contribution does this make to the meaning of the passage? Does the "thousand years" stand in contrast to a period of time that is *less* than what God has determined? It is no wonder that even amillennialist Stanley Grenz finds the traditional amillennial understandings of the thousand years to be unsatisfying (Grenz 1992: 10).

Chilton compares the symbolic use of the "thousand years" in Revelation 20 to the hyperbolic statement, "I've told you a million times!" (Chilton 1987: 507). But even here the analogy breaks down too quickly to lend any support to the symbolic understanding of the "thousand years." First, this use of the number "million" clearly possesses the two characteristics of symbolic language discussed above which are lacking in John's use of "thousand years" in Revelation 20: (a) It possesses a degree of *absurdity* when taken literally, for who has ever told anyone anything a *million* times?, and (b) It possesses a degree of *clarity* when taken symbolically, for it effectively communicates that the speaker believes that he has told his hearer this information over and over again (i.e., a whole lot of times!). This statement ("I've told you a million times!"), unlike the statements in Revelation 20, clearly contains the use of a number that is not to be taken literally. Second, it makes perfect sense to use the hyperbolic "million" when referring to something that has occurred many times (and yet probably less than 100), but how does the symbolic use of "one thousand years" effectively communicate the "great vastness" of a time period that is presently almost *two* thousand years (and still growing) as Chilton says it does (ibid., 506)? Isn't that a little like a mother saying her to son, "I've told you *ten times* to take out the garbage!," in order to emphasize to him the large number of times she had given him this instruction, when in reality she had actually told him this *23* times? Put simply, symbolic understanding of the "thousand years" finds no support in a appeal to the hyperbolic statement, "I've told you a million times!"

[44] Because the millennial kingdom in postmillennialism does not extend throughout the entire period of time between the first and second comings of Christ, a literal interpretation

of the thousand years is not necessarily incompatible with postmillennialism.

Chapter 6: The Millennial Reign of Jesus Christ

[45] Hendriksen 1967: 230-31; Hamilton 1955: 135-36; Hoekema 1979: 230, 235; Hughes 1973: 285, 302; and Venema 2000: 328-30.

[46] There are three primary arguments advanced by amillennialists, who believe that this reign takes place in heaven instead of on earth. First, it is said that only three of the 47 references to "throne" in the book of Revelation refer to some place other than heaven (2:13; 13:2; 16:10) (Venema 2000: 328; Hoekema 1979: 230; Hendriksen 1967: 230). Therefore, to see the thrones as located on the earth "would be inconsistent with the imagery of the book" (Venema 2000: 329). As Thomas notes, however, "such a generalization is not decisive enough to be determinative in every single case" (Thomas 1995: 417). What *is* determinative is the context, which points strongly to thrones upon the earth.

Second, "the fact that the Apostle John speaks of the 'souls' of those who had been beheaded because of the testimony of Jesus adds to the likelihood that the scene is a heavenly one" (Venema 2000: 329; Hughes 1973: 302). Two points can be made in response. First, the word "soul" is used many times in Scripture simply to refer to a person, i.e., "a living creature" or "that which possesses life or a soul" (Bauer, Arndt, and Gingrich, 1979: 894, who list 13 such uses in the New Testament: Mark 3:4; Luke 6:9; 9:56; Acts 2:41, 43; 3:23; 7:14; 27:37; Rom 2:9; 13:1; 1 Cor 15:45; 1 Pet 3:20; and Rev 16:3). Second, and more importantly, the meaning here is dependent on the correct interpretation of the first resurrection, which—as demonstrated in chapter 5—refers to a *bodily* resurrection.

Third, according to Hendriksen, the location of the millennial reign must be where Jesus lives, and Revelation 5 and 12 indicate that He lives in heaven (Hendriksen 1967: 231). The problem with this argument is that it presupposes Christ is not on earth during the millennial reign. In other words, it presupposes that because Christ is in heaven in Revelation 5 and 12, He must be in heaven in Revelation 20 as well.

[47] This promise of the land is referred to throughout Genesis, Exodus, and Deuteronomy—Genesis 12:1, 7; 13:15, 17; 15:7, 18; 17:8; 22:17; 24:7; 26:3-5; 28:13, 15; 35:12; 46:3-4; 48:4; 50:24; Exodus 3:8, 17; 6:6-9; 23:23-33; 34:24 (Kaiser 1998: 226); Deuteronomy 1:8, 36; 6:10, 18, 23; 7:13; 8:1; 9:5; 10:11; 11:9, 21; 19:8; 26:3, 15; 28:11; 30:20; 31:7; and 34:4 (Kaiser 1981: 305).

[48] Although the word "covenant" does not occur in 2 Samuel 7:8-16 and 1 Chronicles 17:7-15, "the biblical expositions of the passage (cf. 2 Sam 23:5; Pss 89:35; 132:12) make it clear that it provides the initial delineation of the Davidic Covenant (Grisanti 1999: 236).

[49] For example, God has already blessed Abraham, made his name great, and made him a great nation.

[50] Although some interpreters see only one group of people in this verse—the martyrs—as MacLeod points out, the martyrs are not mentioned until later in the verse after John had already seen the thrones and their occupants" (MacLeod 2000: 54).

[51] The closest and most reasonable antecedent of "they" in the verb translated "they sat" in verse 4 is "the armies which are in heaven, clothed in fine linen, white and clean" in Revelation 19:14, that is, God's redeemed people (MacLeod 2000: 55). As Thomas writes, "It is an unwavering principle that those who win a war become the ones who assume the rulership over the conquered entity. The enthroned ones must be those who have already risen from the dead and been judged. The only ones who fit this description are those composing the Lamb's bride (19:7-8) and the warrior-King's armies (19:14, 19)....This is the very promise given to members of Christ's bride earlier in the book (2:26-28; 3:12, 21). So the best solution is to identify the subject of ['they sat'] as members of the army of Christ that accompany Him at His return" (Thomas 1995: 414).

[52] As Thomas notes, the judgment here is not one of determining men's eternal destinies, but rather a judgment in the course of history (cf. Dan 7:22, a verse to which Rev 20:4 probably alludes) (Thomas 1995: 414). In other words, this judgment refers to "the power of administration in the sense of a divine commission to act for Christ in the kingdom" (Allen

1999: 484) and is practically synonymous with the concept of reigning with Christ in verses 4 and 6.

[53] According to Thomas, "The function of being 'priests of God and of Christ,' referred to also in 1:6 and 5:10, will not be primarily the impartation of knowledge to [the nations] during the period of Satan's imprisonment, but rather will consist of the privileges of unlimited access to and intimate fellowship with God" (Thomas 1995: 422). Allen understands the role as priests in a broader manner than Thomas, stating that these individuals "will not only have the privilege of intimate access to God and Christ but in the administration of the kingdom they will act in a mediatorial capacity as 'priests of God and of Christ'" (Allen 1999: 486).

[54] "They will join Christ in ruling the earth, but in what way this will be is not known" (Thomas 1995: 422).

[55] As Kaiser notes, "The ownership of the land (as a gift from God) is certain and eternal, but the occupation of it by any given generation is conditioned on obedience" (Kaiser 1981: 307; idem 1978: 94).

[56] As Kaiser writes, "Nowhere can it be shown that most, all, or even some of the promises made to Abraham, Isaac, Jacob, or David, have been nullified, modified, exchanged, or transformed in value. They are abiding as the present heaven and earth; in other words, as lasting as the historical process is prior to the introduction of the eternal state" (Kaiser 1992: 116).

[57] As Saucy notes, "Numerous predictions of a final restoration are found among the later prophets, both before and after the Exile" (Saucy 1993: 223). These include the following: Isaiah 2:2-4; 11:1-16; 14:1-2; 27:1-13; 35:1, 10; 43:5-6; 49:8-13; 59:15b-21; 62:4-7; 66:10-20; Jeremiah 3:11-20; 12:14-17; 16:10-18; 23:1-8; 24:5-7; 30:1-3, 10-11; 31:2-14; 32:36-44; Ezekiel 11:14-20; 20:33-44; 28:25-26; 34:11-16, 23-31; 36:16-36; 37:1-28; 39:21-29; Hosea 1:10-11; 2:14-23; 14:4-7; Joel 3:18-21; Amos 9:11-15; Obadiah 17, 21; Micah 4:6-7; 7:14-20; Zephaniah 3:14-20; Zechariah 8:7-8; 10:6-12; and 14:11.

Many interpreters deny that these passages speak of a future restoration of the nation of Israel, asserting instead that Yahweh fulfilled these promises in the returns from exile under

Zerubbabel (536 B.C.), Ezra (557 B.C.), or Nehemiah (445 B.C.). Several factors, however, render this impossible.

First, several of these restoration passages speak of a restoration in which the ten tribes of the north are reunited with the two tribes of the south (Isa 11:12; Jer 3:18; 23:5-8; 31:27; Ezek 37:15-23; Hosea 1:11; Zech 10:6), and this did not happen under the three previous returns from exile (Kaiser 1992: 105-07; idem 1998: 216; Jelinek 1998: 242). In addition, many of the exiled Jews refused to return to the land or had to be persuaded to do so when the time came (ibid.)—a far cry from what is anticipated in the promises of restoration.

Second, several of these passages speak of the spiritual renewal and wholehearted and consistent obedience of the nation (Deut 30:1-10; Jer 3:17; 24:7; 32:36-44; Ezek 11:14-20; 36:24-38), and this cannot be reconciled with the sinful state of the nation at the time of the previous returns (Kaiser 1992: 105-07; Rooker 1992: 127). As Rooker notes, the books of Nehemiah and Malachi, in particular, point out the many sins of the Israelite community after the return from exile, including intermarriage, non-prescribed offerings, withholding tithes and offerings, immoral priests, and negligence. From the perspective of the postexilic community, then, the fulfillment of the spiritual transformation described by Ezekiel and the other prophets lay in the future (ibid.).

Third, according to some of these texts, the restoration of Israel will be so astounding that it will overshadow in significance the exodus out of Egypt and make it seem small in comparison (Jer 16:14-15; 23:5-8), and such was clearly not the case with the previous returns (see Kaiser 1992: 108; idem 1998: 224).

Fourth, "there are anticipations of future elements of a national restoration present in books as late as Zechariah, which clearly indicate that, although many in Israel did return to the land, there is still a sense in which Israel awaited a wholistic national regathering" (see Zech 10:6-12) (Jelinek 1998: 242; cf. Kaiser 1998: 213). In other words, "if the postexilic returns to the land fulfilled this promised restoration predicted by the prophets, why then did Zechariah continue to announce a still future return (10:8–12) in words that were peppered with the phrases and formulas of such prophecies as Isaiah 11:11 and Jeremiah 50:19?" (Kaiser 1981: 309).

Fifth, according to Zechariah 10:8, at the time of the promised return to the land the Jews will be as numerous as they were prior to the exile, but "the population of the postexilic period was shockingly small" (Kaiser 1998: 215).

Sixth, according to Jeremiah 30:10-11, Yahweh will destroy the nations to which He has scattered the Jews at the time that He restores the nation of Israel, but this did not happen in the previous returns.

Seventh, this promised return to the land is presented as an integral part of the New Covenant (Ezek 36:24-36; Isa 59:15b-21), which could not have been inaugurated prior to Christ.

Eighth, according to Ezekiel 36:16-38, God's purpose for the promised return is the vindication of His name among the nations, and this purpose was not met in the previous returns.

Other interpreters understand these promises to be fulfilled in the eternal state. This, too, fails to account for the biblical data. As Jelinek writes, "It will not do to refer the fulfillment of many of these prophecies to the eternal state when all people already know God, for passages such as Isaiah 2:2-4 and 51:4 teach that the nations will assemble in Zion to learn the Word of God and His ways. A particular people, whether national Israel or the church, could not serve the mediating function of bringing societal deliverance and salvation to other peoples in the eternal state where such a task is unneeded" (Jelinek 1998: 242). This view also fails to take into account that God's purpose in Israel's restoration is that His name be vindicated among the nations (Ezek 36:16-38). How is God's name vindicated among the nations when believers die and go to heaven? The view that understands Ezekiel 36:16-38 to be fulfilled in the eternal state simply does not do justice to the text as it reads in its own context.

The deeper question, of course, is a hermeneutical one. Jelinek's insights are helpful: "What is revealed at first in Scripture (or precedes in God's revelation) is not contradicted by what follows in Scripture. What OT authors wrote had a comprehensible meaning for their contemporary audiences and has a revelatory significance in its own right. What these audiences understood depended on both the prophetic message itself and the previously revealed prophetic messages from God. It is a problematic hermeneutic that must either resignify the OT message or see some aspect of an OT theme reiterated in the NT before it can lend legitimacy or permanency to its relevance. Language that says one thing concerning authorial intention but actually means something else is some form of allegory" (Jelinek 1998: 232).

Jelinek continues: "A historically sensitive study reveals that the NT develops OT teaching as divine history progresses, but the teaching of the OT is not lost in the process. Promises that are made to Israel, therefore, must be fulfilled by God. God can do more than He promised, but He cannot do less. The primary question the exegete of texts on the land of Israel must ask is, Do I have sufficient biblical data to indicate that God is doing more or less than He promised with respect to the land promises to Israel? At least the original promises concerning the land must be fulfilled, lest God be found unfaithful" (ibid.).

[58] "The question as to whether the return follows a national spiritual awakening and turning to the Lord or vice versa is difficult. Sometimes the prophets seem to favor the first, as in Deuteronomy 30, and sometimes it appears that the return precedes any general repentance, as in Ezekiel 36:1–37:14 and perhaps in Isaiah 11. But there can be no question about a future return in any of the prophets" (Kaiser 1981: 309; cf. Jelinek 1998: 239).

[59] That Jesus reigns from Jerusalem is seen not only in the Old Testament prophecies, but also in Revelation 20:9, where He and the saints are found in the beloved city, Jerusalem.

Chapter 7: The Chronology of Revelation 19-20

[60] This significance is recognized and captured well by amillennialist Anthony Hoekema, who writes, "If...one thinks of Revelation 20 as setting forth what follows chronologically after what has been described in chapter 19, one would indeed conclude that the millennium of Revelation 20:1-6 will come after the return of Christ" (Hoekema 1979: 226; cf. idem 1977: 156).

Some amillennialists believe that "the book of Revelation consists of seven sections which run parallel to each other, each of which depicts the church and the world from the time of Christ's first coming to the time of his second coming" (Hoekema 1979: 223; cf. Hendriksen 1967: 22-31). This method of interpretation, called *progressive parallelism*, identifies these seven sections as being found in chapters 1-3, 4-7, 8-11, 12-14, 15-16, 17-19, and 20-22. While this approach is plagued by various difficulties, the narrower question to be considered here is whether or not there is a chronological break between chapters 19 and 20.

⁶¹ It should be noted that a few postmillennialists see a sequential relationship between chapters 19 and 20, but these postmillennialists do not believe that Revelation 19:11-19 refers to the Second Coming of Christ.

⁶² When it is used temporally with a negative particle (as it is here: *me...eti*), *eti* denotes the interruption of something that is already taking place (Ostella 1975: 236-38; cf. Bauer, Arndt, and Gingrich 1979: 315; Abbott-Smith 1986: 183).

⁶³ This is along the lines of a narrative that refers for several chapters to a dog barking at a cat, and is then followed by chapter 20, which begins with the statement, "A man took the dog and locked it in the garage so that the dog would bark at the cat *no longer*." The repeated references to the dog barking—in combination with the purpose statement that the dog would bark *no longer*—indicate a sequential relationship between the earlier chapters and chapter 20 of the hypothetical narrative.

⁶⁴ Two additional objections come from White: (1) The motif of angelic ascent and descent in Revelation 7:2; 10:1; 18:1; and 20:1 substantiates the idea of recapitulation in chapter 20. (2) A careful consideration of the texts shows that the battle of Revelation 20:7-10 is a recapitulation of the one in Revelation 19:17-21 (White 1989: 319-44). See Hoehner 1992: 258-62, for a response to these objections, and see White 1994: 539-51, for a response to Hoehner's response.

⁶⁵ This is the view of Mounce (1977: 353) and Ladd (1972: 263).

⁶⁶ This is the view of Hoehner (1992: 258), Thomas (1995: 410-11; 1992: 132-34), Powell (2001: 6) and Walvoord (1986: 233). According to this view, after a substantial period of the existence of Christ's kingdom on earth, "Satan is able to muster an enormous army of those who have apparently resented Christ's authority over human affairs" and proceeds to deceive them and gather them for battle (vv. 7-8) (Thomas 1992: 132). They are defeated and Satan is thrown into the lake of fire to be tormented forever and ever (vv. 9-10).

This view has been widely ignored by non-premillennialists. According to White, the *only* premillennial attempt to solve this problem "has been to posit that the nations of 20:3

are survivors of the battle in 19:19-21" (White 1989: 323). Hamilton writes, "Since no wicked nations exist on earth at the beginning of the alleged millennium, having all been sent to eternal punishment; since the righteous cannot fall into sin and cannot bear children; and since the wicked dead have not yet been raised according to the premillennialists, just whom could Satan gather to war against the saints?" (Hamilton 1955: 137). According to Riddlebarger, "if premillennialism is correct, then it is glorified saints follow [sic] Satan and revolt against Christ!" (Riddlebarger 1994: 17) Later, Riddlebarger insists that "the supposed apostasy of glorified believers in a future millennial age poses a very difficult problem for all forms of premillennialism" (ibid.: 18). Each of these critiques of the premillennial interpretation of Revelation 20 reflects an ignorance of the view that the nations of verses 3 and 8 will arise from the offspring of non-glorified believers who originally enter the millennium.

[67] Incidentally, the one who regards the mingling of glorified and non-glorified people as an incongruity needs only to remember that the resurrected and glorified Christ lived among (and even ate with) His non-glorified disciples for forty days (Luke 24:43; Acts 1:3) (McClain 1974: 501; Grudem 1994: 1120).

[68] This is the view of Thomas (1995: 424), Walvoord (1966: 303-04), Allen (1999: 489-90), and Hoehner (1992: 258). According to these writers, the differences between the two battles include the following: (1) In Ezekiel the invaders come from the north, but in Revelation they come from "the four corners of the earth" (i.e., from all directions). (2) In Ezekiel 38:2 Gog and Magog are identified only as a local northern power, but in Revelation they refer to all the nations. (3) In Ezekiel Gog is a prince and Magog is the land that contains Rosh, Meshech, and Tubal, but in Revelation Gog and Magog are all the nations. (4) In Ezekiel 38:15-16 Gog and Magog go against Israel, but in Revelation they go against the saints and Jerusalem. (5) In Ezekiel 39:4 and 17 the invaders fall upon Israel's mountains, but in Revelation they are devoured by fire from heaven. (6) In Ezekiel 39:17-20, there is a great feast of corpses after the battle, but in Revelation the invaders are consumed by fire. (7) In Ezekiel the invaders are led by Gog, but in Revelation they are led by Satan. (8) In Ezekiel the invasion comes at the beginning of Christ's millennial reign, but in Revelation it comes at the end.

[69] This is the view of Mounce, who writes, "It is worth noting that in Ezekiel and Revelation the assault *follows* the period of the messianic kingdom. In Ezekiel 36-37 Israel is restored to the land; then comes the warfare in chapters 38 and 39" (Mounce 1977: 361). According to MacLeod, there are at least six different views on the timing of the invasion of Ezekiel 38-39: (1) The invasion will take place before the Tribulation. (2) The invasion will take place in the middle of the Tribulation. (3) The events will take place at the end of the Tribulation. (4) The events of Ezekiel 38-39 will spread over a period of time, with chapter 38 being fulfilled in the middle of the Tribulation and chapter 39 being fulfilled at its end. (5) The invasion will take place at the end of the millennium. (6) Ezekiel's prophecy will be fulfilled in two events, one recorded in Revelation 19:17-21 and one in Revelation 20:7-10 (MacLeod 2000: 208).

Chapter 8: Satan's Final Battle

[70] Amillennialists generally understand Revelation 20:8-9 to refer to a persecution of the church at the end of the present age (the war) that is terminated by the glorious return of Christ (the fire coming down from heaven).

[71] The use of "Gog and Magog" is most likely an allusion to Ezekiel 38 and 39, where Gog is a prince and Magog is the land that contains Rosh, Meshech, and Tubal. See chapter 7 for a discussion of whether or not the battle in Revelation 20:7-10 is the same as the one in Ezekiel. If the battles are the same, John's use of "Gog and Magog" makes perfect sense. If the battles are not the same, however, it could be that "the Gog and Magog 'legend' is applied to a new historical situation (20:8), with Satan leading the new 'Gog and Magog'" (MacLeod 2000: 209). This could be likened to referring to the terrorist attacks on September 11, 2001 as the "Pearl Harbor" of our day.

[72] MacLeod writes, "Many of those who will be born to Christian parents will not acknowledge Christ as their Savior, but will remain in unbelief, and many will chafe under His rule. So when Satan seeks to seduce them into rebellion, they will readily follow him" (MacLeod 2000: 207).

[73] Some interpreters have understood the term "camp" to refer to a military camp and believe it indicates that the saints are expecting the attack and are therefore poised to defend Jerusalem (MacLeod 2000: 210). According to Thomas, however, "since the saints have no part in repelling the attackers and have no occasion to be organized as a military unit, the meaning probably aligns more closely with usage of the noun in the LXX to speak of the camp of the Israelites (e.g., Ex. 16:13, 29:14; Deut. 23:14; Heb. 13:11, 13). It refers simply to a place of dwelling for the saints" (Thomas 1995: 425).

[74] See Genesis 19:24; Leviticus 10:2; Ezekiel 38:22; 39:6; 2 Kings 1:10, 12; and Luke 9:54 (Thomas 1995: 425-26). If the fire here in Revelation 20:9 is symbolic, it seems to indicate a lopsided victory due to divine intervention.

[75] The question of whether "the lake of fire" includes literal fire will be taken up in chapter nine.

[76] According to Allen, "The expression 'day and night' (4:8; 7:15; 12:10; 14:11) is a common metaphorical way of expressing something that goes on endlessly or ceaselessly—there is never any intermission" (Allen 1999: 493). As Thomas notes, "This is a figure of speech based on the experience of our earthly time frame" (Thomas 1995: 427).

[77] According to Allen, this phrase "is the strongest possible expression in the Greek language to express emphatically that the punishment lasts eternally" (Allen 1999: 493). That consignment to the lake of fire does not involve annihilation is further suggested by the fact that, at this point, the beast and the false prophet have already been there for one thousand years.

Chapter 9: In the Courtroom of God

[78] That Revelation 20:11c carries this meaning is corroborated by the use of similar language in Revelation 6:14 and 16:20.

[79] That this judgment has reference only to unbelievers is indicated by the following considerations: (1) "The rest of the dead" in verse 5—which refers to unbelievers—is the obvious antecedent of "the dead" in verse 12. (2) The resurrection of

"the dead" in verses 11-13 is the "second resurrection" implied in verse 5b, and this "second resurrection" leads to the "second death" in verse 6a, of which believers are said to have no part (Thomas 1995: 431). (3) The only stated outcome of this judgment is the lake of fire (20:15). (4) "The Book of Life comes into the discussion only to show that the names of these dead are not written there" (ibid.). (5) This fits the context of Revelation 19-20, which sets forth God's victory over everything tainted by sin—the beast, the false prophet, Satan, heaven and earth, and now His unbelieving human enemies.

[80] In its eleven uses in the New Testament (Matt 11:23; 16:18; Luke 10:15; 16:23; Acts 2:27, 31; 1 Cor 15:55; Rev 1:18; 6:8; 20:13, 14), "Hades" is used to refer either to (1) the place of the bodies of the dead (i.e., the grave) (e.g., Acts 2:27) or (2) the intermediate state where the souls of the wicked are tormented (e.g., Luke 16:23). While neither of these two is definitively precluded by the context of Revelation 20, the evidence indicates that its use in verses 13 and 14 refers to the grave. First, for John to refer to the bodies of those lost at sea but not those buried in graves would be surprising. Second, although the soul *is* reunited with the body at the time of a resurrection, the emphasis in this context seems to be on the resurrection of the body. Third, the casting of "Hades" into the lake of fire in verse 14 most naturally refers to the destruction of (physical) death (cf. Rev 21:4). And fourth, when "Hades" is paired up with "death" elsewhere in Revelation (1:18 and 6:8), the two seem to refer to physical death.

[81] At the same time, it may be stated in response that although literal fire would quickly burn up an ordinary human body, those in hell will not have ordinary human bodies. "They will be resurrected bodily, and just as the redeemed will have bodies uniquely suited for glory, these will have bodies uniquely suited for judgment." (MacLeod 2000: 212-13).

[82] The word translated "of fire" (*puros*) is most likely a genitive of *content* (see Wallace 1996: 92-94), which means that the fire is the *content* that fills the lake. Instead of a lake filled with *water*, then, John speaks of a lake filled with *fire*.

[83] This is also suggested by the words of Christ in Matthew 10:28: "And do not fear those who kill the body, but are

unable to kill the soul; but rather fear Him who is able to destroy both soul and body in hell." As Wallace writes, "What is important to note here is that the place of the destruction of the body is hell" (Wallace 2001: 2). Incidentally, in this article Wallace is not arguing for literal fire *per se*, but rather that the punishment of hell will be both spiritual *and* physical.

[84] That those punished in the lake of fire are punished *eternally* (rather than annihilated) is further implied by Revelation 20:10, which says that after one thousand years in the lake of fire, the beast and the false prophet were still being tormented there.

Bibliography

Abbott-Smith, G.

1986   *A Manual Greek Lexicon of the New Testament.* Edinburgh: T. & T. Clark Ltd.

Allen, James.

1999   *Revelation.* What the Bible Teaches: Ritchie New Testament Commentaries. Edited by T. Wilson and K. Stapley. Kilmarnock: John Ritchie Ltd.

Augustine.

1950   *The City of God.* Translated by Marcus Dods. New York: The Modern Library.

Barbieri, Louis A., Jr.

1983   "Matthew." In *The Bible Knowledge Commentary: An Exposition of the Scriptures by Dallas Seminary Faculty, New Testament Edition.* Edited by John F. Walvoord and Roy B. Zuck, 13-94. Wheaton: Victor Books.

Bauer, Walter, William F. Arndt, and Wilbur Gingrich.

1979   *A Greek-English Lexicon of the New Testament and Other Early Christian Literature.* 2nd ed. Revised and augmented by F. Wilbur Gingrich and Frederick W. Danker. Chicago: University of Chicago Press.

Beasley-Murray, G. R.

1974   *The Book of Revelation*. New Century Bible. Edited by G. R. Beasley-Murray. Greenwood: The Attic Press, Inc.

Beckwith, Isbon T.

1922   *The Apocalypse of John*. New York: The MacMillan Company.

Bellshaw, William G.

1968   "The New Testament Doctrine of Satan," *Grace Journal* 9:24-39.

Berkhof, Louis

1939   *Systematic Theology*. Grand Rapids: William B. Eerdmans Publishing Company.

Blaising, Craig A. and Darrell L. Bock

1993   *Progressive Dispensationalism*. Wheaton: Victor Books.

Blaising, Craig A.

1999   "A Premillennial Response to Robert B. Strimple." In *Three Views on the Millennium and Beyond*. Edited by Darrell L. Bock, 143-53. Grand Rapids: Zondervan Publishing House.

1999   "A Premillennial Response to Kenneth L. Gentry Jr." In *Three Views on the Millennium and Beyond*. Edited by Darrell L. Bock, 72-80. Grand Rapids: Zondervan Publishing House.

1999   "Premillennialism." In *Three Views on the Millennium and Beyond*. Edited by Darrell L. Bock, 157-227. Grand Rapids: Zondervan Publishing House.

Blomberg, Craig

1992   *Matthew*. In The New American Commentary. Edited by David S. Dockery. Nashville: Broadman Press.

1998   "Eschatology and the Church: Some New Testament Perspectives." *Themelios* 23:3-26.

Bock, Darrell L.

1996   *Luke 9:51-24:53*. In Baker Exegetical Commentary on the New Testament. Edited by Moises Silva. Grand Rapids: Baker Books.

1999   "Summary Essay." In *Three Views on the Millennium and Beyond*. Edited by Darrell L. Bock, 279-309. Grand Rapids: Zondervan Publishing House.

Boer, Harry R.

1975   "What about the Millennium?" *Reformed Journal* 25.

Boettner, Loraine

1957   *The Millennium*. Philadephia: The Presbyterian and Reformed Publishing Company.

1977   "A Postmillennial Response." In *The Meaning of the Millennium: Four Views*. Edited by Robert G. Clouse, 199-208. Downers Grove: InterVarsity Press.

Broadus, John Albert

1886   *Commentary on the Gospel of Matthew*. Philadelphia: American Baptist Publication Society.

Bruce, Alexander Balmain

1974   "The Synoptic Gospels." In *The Expositor's Greek Testament*, vol. 1. Edited by W. Robertson Nicoll. Grand Rapids: William B. Eerdmans Publishing Company.

Carson, D. A., Douglas J. Moo, and Leon Morris

1992   *An Introduction to the New Testament*. Grand Rapids: Zondervan.

Chilton, David

1987   *The Days of Vengeance: An Exposition of the Book of Revelation*. Fort Worth: Dominion Press.

Cohen, Gary G.

1978   *Understanding Revelation: An Investigation of the Key Interpretational and Chronological Questions Which Surround the Book of Revelation*. Chicago: Moody Press.

Cox, William E.
1966   *Amillennialism Today*. Phillipsburg: Presbyterian and Reformed Publishing Company.

Crockett, William V.
1992   "Response to John F. Walvoord." In *Four Views on Hell*. Edited by William V. Crockett, 29-31. Grand Rapids: Zondervan Publishing House.

1992   "The Metaphorical View." In *Four Views on Hell*. Edited by William V. Crockett, 43-76. Grand Rapids: Zondervan Publishing House.

Davis, John J.
1941   *Biblical Numerology*. Grand Rapids: William B. Eerdmans Publishing Company.

Deere, Jack S.
1978   "Premillennialism in Revelation 20:4-6." *Bibliotheca Sacra* 135:58-73.

Erickson, Millard J.
1998   *A Basic Guide to Eschatology: Making Sense of the Millennium*. Grand Rapids: Baker Books.

Feinberg, Charles L.
1980   *Millennialism: The Two Major Views*, 3rd ed. Chicago: Moody Press.

Garlington, Donald
1997   "Reigning with Christ: Revelation 20:1-6 and the Question of the Millennium." *Reformation & Revival* 6:53-100.

Gentry, Kenneth L. Jr.
1998   "A Preterist View of Revelation." In *Four Views on the Book of Revelation*. Edited by C. Marvin Pate, 37-92. Grand Rapids: Zondervan Publishing House.

1999   "A Postmillennial Response to Craig A. Blaising." In *Three Views on the Millennium and Beyond*. Edited by Darrell L. Bock, 228-55. Grand Rapids: Zondervan Publishing House.

1999   "A Postmillennial Response to Robert B. Strimple." In *Three Views on the Millennium and Beyond*.

Edited by Darrell L. Bock, 130-42. Grand Rapids: Zondervan Publishing House.

1999   "Postmillennialism." In *Three Views on the Millennium and Beyond*. Edited by Darrell L. Bock, 13-57. Grand Rapids: Zondervan Publishing House.

Green, Joel B.

1997   *The Gospel of Luke*. In The New International Commentary on the New Testament. Edited by Gordon D. Fee. Grand Rapids: William B. Eerdmans Publishing Company.

Green, Michael

1987   *2 Peter and Jude*. In Tyndale New Testament Commentaries. Edited by Leon Morris. Grand Rapids: William B. Eerdmans Publishing Company.

Gregg, Steve, ed.

1997   *Revelation, Four Views: A Parallel Commentary*. Nashville: Thomas Nelson Publishers.

Grenz, Stanely J.

1992   *The Millennial Maze: Sorting Out Evangelical Options*. Downers Grove: InterVarsity Press.

Grisanti, Michael A.

1999   "The Davidic Covenant." *The Master's Seminary Journal* 10:233-50.

Grudem, Wayne

1994   *Systematic Theology: An Introduction to Biblical Doctrine*. Grand Rapids: Zondervan.

Hamilton, Floyd E.

1955   *The Basis of Millennial Faith*. Grand Rapids: William B. Eerdmans Publishing Company.

Hamstra, Sam Jr.

1998   "An Idealist View of Revelation." In *Four Views on the Book of Revelation*. Edited by C. Marvin Pate, 95-131. Grand Rapids: Zondervan Publishing House.

Harris, Gregory H.

1999   "Satan's Deceptive Miracles in the Tribulation." *Bibliotheca Sacra* 156:308-24.

1999   "Satan's Work as Deceiver." *Bibliotheca Sacra*
        156:190-202.

Hartley, John E. and Alice Hickcox

1988   "Snare; Trap." In *International Standard Bible
        Encyclopedia*. Edited by Geoffrey W. Bromiley,
        4:556. Grand Rapids: William B. Eerdmans
        Publishing Company.

Hendriksen, William

1967   *More Than Conquerors: An Interpretation of the
        Book of Revelation*. Grand Rapids: Baker Book
        House.

1978   *Exposition of the Gospel According to Luke*. In New
        Testament Commentary. Grand Rapids: Baker
        Book House.

Hiebert, D. Edmond

1977   *An Introduction to the New Testament, Volume
        Three: The Non-Pauline Epistles and Revelation*.
        Winona Lake: BMH Books.

1989   *Second Peter and Jude: An Expositional Commen-
        tary*. Greenville: Unusual Publications.

1991   *The Epistles of John: An Expositional Commentary*.
        Greenville: Bob Jones University Press.

Hoehner, Harold W.

1992   "Evidence from Revelation 20." In *A Case for Pre-
        millennialism: A New Consensus*. Edited by Donald
        K. Campbell and Jeffrey L. Townsend, 235-62.
        Chicago: Moody Press.

Hoekema, Anthony A.

1977   "Amillennialism." In *The Meaning of the Millen-
        nium: Four Views*. Edited by Robert G. Clouse,
        155-87. Downers Grove: InterVarsity Press.

1977   "An Amillennial Response." In *The Meaning of the
        Millennium: Four Views*. Edited by Robert G.
        Clouse, 55-59. Downers Grove: InterVarsity Press.

1979   *The Bible and the Future*. Grand Rapids: William B.
        Eerdmans Publishing Company.

Hoyt, Herman A.

1977   "A Dispensational Premillennial Response." In *The Meaning of the Millennium: Four Views*. Edited by Robert G. Clouse, 192-98. Downers Grove: Inter-Varsity Press.

1977   "Dispensational Premillennialism." In *The Meaning of the Millennium: Four Views*. Edited by Robert G. Clouse, 63-92. Downers Grove: InterVarsity Press.

Hughes, James A.

1973   "Revelation 20:4-6 and the Question of the Millennium." *Westminster Theological Journal* 35: 281-302.

Jelinek, John A.

1998   "The Dispersion and Restoration of Israel to the Land." In *Israel, the Land and the People: An Evangelical Affirmation of God's Promises*. Edited by H. Wayne House, 231-58. Grand Rapids: Kregel Publications.

Johnson, Alan

1981   "Revelation." In *The Expositor's Bible Commentary*. Edited by Frank E. Gaebelein, 12:399-603. Grand Rapids: Zondervan Publishing House.

Kaiser, Walter C., Jr.

1981   "The Promised Land: A Biblical-Historical View." *Bibliotheca Sacra* 138:302-11.

1992   "Evidence from Jeremiah." In *A Case for Premillennialism: A New Consensus*. Edited by Donald K. Campbell and Jeffrey L. Townsend, 103-17. Chicago: Moody Press.

1998   "The Land of Israel and the Future Return (Zechariah 10:6-12)." In *Israel, the Land and the People: An Evangelical Affirmation of God's Promises*. Edited by H. Wayne House, 209-27. Grand Rapids: Kregel Publications.

Kistemaker, Simon

1987   *Exposition of the Epistles of Peter and of the Epistle of Jude*. In New Testament Commentary. Grand Rapids: Baker Book House.

Kline, Meredith G.
1975   "The First Resurrection." *Westminster Theological Journal* 37 (1974-75): 366-75.

1976   "The First Resurrection: A Reaffirmation." *Westminster Theological Journal* 39: 110-19.

Knight, George W., III
1992   *The Pastoral Epistles: A Commentary on the Greek Text*. The New International Greek Testament Commentary. Edited by I. Howard Marshall and W. Ward Gasque. Grand Rapids: Eerdmans.

Ladd, George Eldon
1952   *Crucial Questions About the Kingdom of God*. Grand Rapids: William B. Eerdmans Publishing Company.

1960   "Revelation 20 and the Millennium," *Review and Expositor* 57:167-75.

1972   *A Commentary on the Revelation of John*. Grand Rapids: William B. Eerdmans Publishing Company.

1977   "An Historic Premillennial Response." In *The Meaning of the Millennium: Four Views*. Edited by Robert G. Clouse, 189-91. Downers Grove: InterVarsity Press.

1977   "Historic Premillennialism." In *The Meaning of the Millennium: Four Views*. Edited by Robert G. Clouse, 17-40. Downers Grove: InterVarsity Press.

Lewis, Arthur H.
1980   *The Dark Side of the Millennium: The Problem of Evil in Revelation 20:10*. Grand Rapids: Baker Book House.

Liefeld, Walter L.
1976   "Abyss." In *The Zondervan Pictorial Encyclopedia of the Bible*. Edited by Merrill C. Tenney, 3:30-31. Grand Rapids: Zondervan Publishing House.

Louw, Johannes P. and Eugene A. Nida, eds.
1989   *Greek-English Lexicon of the New Testament Based on Semantic Domains*. 2 vols. 2nd ed. New York: United Bible Societies.

MacArthur, John

2000   *Revelation 12-22*. The MacArthur New Testament Commentary. Chicago: Moody Press.

MacLeod, David J.

1999   "The Second 'Last Thing': The Defeat of Antichrist (Rev. 19:17-21)." *Bibliotheca Sacra* 156:325-35.

1999   "The Third 'Last Thing': The Binding of Satan (Rev. 20:1-3)." *Bibliotheca Sacra* 156:469-86.

2000   "The Fifth 'Last Thing': The Release of Satan and Man's Final Rebellion (Rev. 20:7-10)." *Bibliotheca Sacra* 157:200-14.

2000   "The Fourth 'Last Thing': The Millennial Kingdom of Christ (Rev. 20:4-6)." *Bibliotheca Sacra* 157:44-67.

McClain, Alva J.

1974   *The Greatness of the Kingdom: An Inductive Study of the Kingdom of God*. Winona Lake: BMH Books.

Michaels, J. R.

1976   "The First Resurrection: A Response." *Westminster Theological Journal* 39:100-09.

Moo, Douglas J.

1996   *The Epistle to the Romans*. In The New International Commentary on the New Testament. Edited by Gordon D. Fee. Grand Rapids: William B. Eerdmans Publishing Company.

Morris, Leon

1987   *Revelation*. In Tyndale New Testament Commentaries. Edited by Leon Morris. Grand Rapids: William B. Eerdmans Publishing Company.

Moulton, James Hope

1908   *A Grammar of New Testament Greek*. Edinburgh: T. & T. Clark.

Mounce, Robert H.

1977   *The Book of Revelation*. New International Commentary on the New Testament. Edited by F. F. Bruce. Grand Rapids: William B. Eerdmans Publishing Company.

Ostella, Richard A.

1975 "The Significance of Deception in Revelation 20:3," *Westminster Theological Journal* 37:236-38.

Page, Sydney H. T.

1980 "Revelation 20 and Pauline Eschatology," *Journal of the Evangelical Theological Society* 23:31-43.

Pate, C. Marvin.

1998 "A Progressive Dispensationalist View of Revelation." In *Four Views on the Book of Revelation.* Edited by C. Marvin Pate, 135-75. Grand Rapids: Zondervan Publishing House.

1998 "Introduction to Revelation." In *Four Views on the Book of Revelation.* Edited by C. Marvin Pate, 9-34. Grand Rapids: Zondervan Publishing House.

Plummer, Alfred

1975 *A Critical and Exegetical Commentary on the Gospel According to S. Luke.* In The International Critical Commentary. Edited by Alfred Plummer, Samuel Rolles Driver, and Charles Augustus Briggs. Edinburgh: T. & T. Clark.

Powell, Charles E.

2001 "Progression Versus Recapitulation in Revelation 20:1-6: Some Overlooked Arguments." http://www.bible.org/docs/soapbox/scholars/rev20.htm, January.

Poythress, Vern Sheridan

1993 "Genre and Hermeneutics in Rev 20:1-6," *Journal of the Evangelical Theological Society* 36:41-54.

2000 *The Returning King: A Guide to the Book of Revelation.* Phillipsburg: P&R Publishing.

Rainbow, Paul A.

1996 "Millenium as Metaphor in John's Apocalypse," *Westminster Theological Journal* 58:209-21.

Riddlebarger, Kim

1994 "A Present or a Future Millennium?" *modern Reformation* (May/June): 14-18.

Robertson, A. T.

1933   *Word Pictures in the New Testament*. 6 vols. Nashville: Broadman Press.

1934   *A Grammar of the Greek New Testament in the Light of Historical Research*. Nashville: Broadman Press.

Rooker, Mark F.

1992   "Evidence from Ezekiel." In *A Case for Premillennialism: A New Consensus*. Edited by Donald K. Campbell and Jeffrey L. Townsend, 119-134. Chicago: Moody Press.

Saucy, Robert L.

1993   *The Case for Progressive Dispensationalism: The Interface Between Dispensational and Non-Dispensational Theology*. Grand Rapids: Zondervan Publishing House.

Smith, Charles R.

1969   "The New Testament Doctrine of Demons," *Grace Journal* 10:26-41.

Stein, Robert H.

1992   *Luke*. In The New American Commentary. Edited by David S. Dockery. Nashville: Broadman Press.

Strimple, Robert B.

1999   "Amillennialism." In *Three Views on the Millennium and Beyond*. Edited by Darrell L. Bock, 83-129. Grand Rapids: Zondervan Publishing House.

1999   "An Amillennial Response to Craig A. Blaising" In *Three Views on the Millennium and Beyond*. Edited by Darrell L. Bock, 256-76. Grand Rapids: Zondervan Publishing House.

1999   "An Amillennial Response to Kenneth L. Gentry Jr." In *Three Views on the Millennium and Beyond*. Edited by Darrell L. Bock, 58-71. Grand Rapids: Zondervan Publishing House.

Summers, Ray

1960   "Revelation 20: An Interpretation." *Review and Expositor* 57:176-83.

Swete, Henry Barclay
1977   *Commentary on Revelation*. Grand Rapids: Kregel Publications.

Terry, Milton
1898   *Biblical Apocalyptics: A Study of the Most Notable Revelations of God and of Christ in the Canonical Scriptures*. New York: Eaton and Mains.

Thomas, Robert L.
1966   "John's Apocalyptic Outline." *Bibliotheca Sacra* 123:334-341.

1991   "Literary Genre and Hermeneutics of the Apocalypse." *The Master's Seminary Journal* 2:79-97.

1992   *Revelation 1-7: An Exegetical Commentary*. Chicago: Moody Press.

1992   "The Kingdom of Christ in the Apocalypse." *The Master's Seminary Journal* 3:117-40.

1993   "The Structure of the Apocalypse: Recapitulation or Progression?" *The Master's Seminary Journal* 4:45-66.

1994   "Theonomy and the Dating of Revelation." *The Master's Seminary Journal* 5:185-202.

1995   *Revelation 8-22: An Exegetical Commentary*. Chicago: Moody Press.

1998   "A Classical Dispensationalist View of Revelation." In *Four Views on the Book of Revelation*. Edited by C. Marvin Pate, 179-229. Grand Rapids: Zondervan Publishing House.

Townsend, Jeffrey L.
1983   "Is the Present Age the Millennium?" *Bibliotheca Sacra* 140:206-224.

Turner, Nigel
1963   *A Grammar of New Testament Greek*, 4 vols. Edinburgh: T. & T. Clark.

Venema, Cornelis P.
2000   *The Promise of the Future*. Carlisle: The Banner of Truth Trust.

Wallace, Daniel B.

1996   *Greek Grammar Beyond the Basics: An Exegetical Syntax of the New Testament.* Grand Rapids: Zondervan Publishing House.

2001   "Hell: Spiritual or Physical or Both?" http://www.bible.org/docs/soapbox/hell.htm, June.

2002   "Is Intra-Canonical Theological Development Compatible with a High Bibliology?" http://www.bible.org/docs/soapbox/scholars/intra canon.htm, April.

Walvoord, John F.

1959   *The Millennial Kingdom.* Grand Rapids: Zondervan Publishing House.

1966   *The Revelation of Jesus Christ.* Chicago: Moody Press.

1986   "The Theological Significance of Revelation 20:1-6." In *Essays in Honor of J. Dwight Pentecost.* Edited by Stanley D. Toussaint and Charles H. Dyer, 228-38. Chicago: Moody Press.

1992   "The Literal View." In *Four Views on Hell.* Edited by William V. Crockett, 11-28. Grand Rapids: Zondervan Publishing House.

1995   "Is Satan Bound?" In *Vital Prophetic Issues: Examining Promises and Problems in Eschatology.* Edited by Roy B. Zuck, 83-95. Grand Rapids: Kregel Resources.

Warfield, Benjamin B.

1929   *Biblical Doctrines.* New York: Oxford University.

White, R. Fowler

1989   "Reexamining the Evidence for Recapitulation in Rev 20:1-10." *Westminster Theological Journal* 51:319-44.

1994   "Making Sense of Rev 20:1-10? Harold Hoehner Versus Recapitulation." *Journal of the Evangelical Theological Society* 37:539-51.